Jonathan Owen was called to the Bar by Inner Temple in 2004, having completed his undergraduate degree at Magdalen College, Oxford, and the Bar Vocational Course at Nottingham Law School. He is a tenant at Ropewalk Chambers, in Nottingham, where he has practised since completion of pupillage. He has a broad civil practice with a particular focus on personal injury and industrial disease work.

Gareth McAloon was called to the Bar by Lincoln's Inn in 2010. He is a tenant at Ropewalk Chambers, in Nottingham. Gareth specialises in all aspects of personal injury work, predominantly on the Multi-Track. He is a specialist practitioner in all aspects of industrial disease claims including; asbestos claims, NIHL claims, HAVS claims and repetitive strain injuries. In addition, Gareth is instructed in inquests and clinical negligence claims. The high value nature and complexity of the cases he deals with means that he has regular contact with medical and engineering experts both in Court and in his case preparation.

A Practical Guide to Asbestos Claims

A Practical Guide to Asbestos Claims

Jonathan Owen
Barrister, Ropewalk Chambers
MA (Oxon)

Gareth McAloon
Barrister, Ropewalk Chambers
LLB, LLM, BCL (Oxford)

Law Brief Publishing

The information in this book was believed to be correct at the time of writing. All content is for information purposes only and is not intended as legal advice. No liability is accepted by either the publisher or author for any errors or omissions (whether negligent or not) that it may contain. Professional advice should always be obtained before applying any information to particular circumstances.

Published 2020 by Law Brief Publishing, an imprint of Law Brief Publishing Ltd
30 The Parks
Minehead
Somerset
TA24 8BT

www.lawbriefpublishing.com

Paperback: 978-1-913715-24-3

PREFACE

All those who practice in asbestos litigation are privileged, whether they act for the Claimant or the Defendant. It is a field of disease litigation which concerns matters of life and death, where matters must be dealt with sensitively to the context, but properly. It has been a field of ceaseless development by way of judicial authority over the last 20 years. There has always been "*another battle to fight*".In this book we have sought to state the law accurately as it stands as of 31 August 2020. We too have been privileged to write this book.

Jonathan Owen
Gareth McAloon
Ropewalk Chambers
September 2020

CONTENTS

CHAPTER ONE
INTRODUCTION

At the outset of this book is important to acknowledge and impress upon readers, the sensitivity and emotion which will often feature in claims for asbestos-related injury. As is now common knowledge, respiratory conditions arising from asbestos exposure can have devastating, and potentially, fatal consequences. For some, their illness will be incredibly aggressive once symptoms begin to manifest and their suffering will be great. In others, their illness may be less aggressive but one which they will have to live with for many years, during which the time they will have to live with the knowledge that they could face rapid deterioration in their health as a consequence later on. As such, emotions will often run high on the Claimant side and urgent considerations and decisions will need to be on the Defendant side. Accordingly, and in recognition of those considerations, the Courts have developed law, practices and procedures to deal with these types of claims specifically and to stream-line the litigation process to arrive at a finalised outcome as swiftly as possible.

At the time of writing, asbestos litigation remains as one of the forerunners of the Industrial Disease market. Despite the awareness of the severe risks which asbestos exposure poses workers, the legacy of asbestos-related claims continues to span decades. It has often been predicted that the numbers of such claims had 'reached their peak' but the reality is that they continue and the latest figures generated by the insurance industry meeting these claims, has predicted that their peak will not be reached until around 2028. Even after that, the rate of decline in their number will be gradual over the next 10 years or so.

Part of the reason for the continued rate of new claims is the level of ignorance that there was amongst employer's and the slow-reaction rates of successive governments to adequately regulate the use of asbestos in industry in the latter half of the 20th Century. That, almost lethargic, approach, meant that asbestos continued to be widely used across a variety of industries until the 1990s.

The other reason is, of course, the nature of asbestos-related conditions which those who have been exposed, go one to suffer. Invariably with such conditions there is a prolonged latency period during which the sufferer has no idea that changes are taking place within their respiratory system which will subsequently adversely affect their health in later years, and in the worst cases, go on to bring their life to an end. There is no 'typical' latency period between exposure and symptoms manifesting themselves to those exposed – it varies from individual to individual. However, what can be said is that there seems to be a minimum period of around 15-20 years and, more often, even longer, particularly in those who have otherwise had relatively good respiratory health which has been unaffected by other conditions such as smoking. Indeed, the average period of onset, is thought to be around 35 years. The net effect of that is ultimately, that Claimant's remain 'injured' in the strictest sense, but totally unaware and asymptomatic for decades until the later years of their life – typically in their 70s and 80s.

Consequently, the coincidence of those two predominant factors, has meant that exposure to asbestos has continued even to the present day and, accordingly, for those who go on to develop an asbestos-related respiratory condition, the chances are that their symptoms will not manifest themselves for many years yet. It is for those reasons that the insurance industry continues to develop and deploy reserves into preparation for future asbestos claims as they come to pass.

The key to dealing with asbestos claims is understanding two core components; firstly, the history of industrial and medical knowledge as it developed throughout the 20th Century. Secondly, being able to deal with causation and the knock-on effects of that issue on the value of claims moving forward.

This booked is aimed predominantly, at the new practitioner in asbestos claims with a view to giving a starting point on those two core issues. Our book is not intended to be a 'chapter and verse' guide to dealing with asbestos claims. Undoubtedly, there are those more detailed texts out there, but rather, we aim to be a quick source of reference for practitioners to grasp the core issues and allow them to properly direct and further, more specific, research that is then required for their specific cases which they have to deal with.

To those ends, therefore, we will start with the very basic aspects of understanding what asbestos is and what it was most commonly used for. We will then go on to outline the industry and medical research and publications which have often been referred to in evidence in those cases which have proceeded before the Courts, and further this discussion in the context of the employer's duty of care which the Courts have then go on to formulate. Next, we will discuss the evidential issues which then arise in asbestos claims and how such evidence informs a Defendant's position on whether or not breach is likely to be established against them or not. We shall them move to the medical aspect and discuss the types of asbestos-conditions which are most commonly the subject of claims for damages and then discuss the legal tests of causation developed by the Courts to determine whether or not such claims ought to proceed in establishing liability. We will then complete our discussions by looking at the more complex issue of determining quantum of damages, particularly, the more vexed issue of dealing with damages in living claims. Finally, we shall then discuss two further matters which have a common bearing on the progress of asbestos claims, firstly; the bespoke procedural framework which asbestos claims are subjected to via Practice Direction 3D, and secondly, limitation defences and common issues which arise in arguing such defences including the discretionary permission available to statute-barred Claimants under Section 33 of the Limitation Act 1980.

CHAPTER TWO
WHAT IS ASBESTOS?

Starting at the most basic of starting points, it is firstly important to understand what asbestos is and what it is, or was, used for most commonly.

(i) What is asbestos?

In short, asbestos is a group of some six naturally occurring silicate minerals which is made up of strand upon strand of tiny microscopic fibres. It is not, in its core form, man-made. The fibres are generally soft and malleable so that they could be moulded into various shapes. It was mined extensively in the latter half of the 19th Century, and this continued in the 20th Century. The most intense mining for asbestos is believed to have taken place in South Africa which was where Amosite production began in the early 19th century. Many other countries had asbestos mines which would export the mineral abroad.

Asbestos was predominantly deployed in the manufacturing and construction industries. The reason for its popularity was predominantly its heat resistance and its ability to be fire retardant. With that, it was also good at keeping heat and can also be used to strengthen other material. Accordingly, asbestos was regularly used as a form of fire-protection or insulation.

(ii) The types of asbestos

Descriptions and images of each type of asbestos are well publicised on the internet and can be easily searched for. Below are some images of the six registered types of asbestos mineral which have now been recognised by nearly every country as a controlled material. The images have been downloaded from various sites which are credited in the footnotes and where more in-depth knowledge as to each can be found.

In the United States, the six types of asbestos fibre are divided into two-groups by The Asbestos Hazard Emergency Response Act 1986[1]. The groups and types of asbestos are:

(a) Amphibole Asbestos

Within this group, the asbestos fibres have straight edges and are quite linear and distinct. As such, when broken the fibres remain jagged and to some extent neat.

The types of asbestos which fall into this category are:

Crocidolite Asbestos : Also known as 'blue asbestos'. This form of asbestos was known to be less heat resistant and therefore was used more as a form of insulation than for fire-protection.

Tremolite : This type of asbestos can come in a variety of colours. But again, it is noticeable for its straight fibres which move in different directions and are interwoven. Tremolite was commonly used in other minerals, most notably, talc, and was used in talcum powder products prior to the 1980s.

Anthophyllite : This form of asbestos saw relatively limited commercial usage. It is usually various shades of brown or grey in colour. Its use was also generally in insultation products.

Amosite : Also known as 'brown asbestos'. Frequently used with cement products and also insulating products. It was also very strong and heat resistant and so was used in ceiling tiles as well.

Actinolite : Similar to Tremolite, this form of asbestos was rarely used commercially but was used in with other mineral based products.

(b) Serpentine Asbestos

Only one category of asbestos falls into this category; chrysotile. The Category is separately created because the fibre structure is different to

1 See: https://www.congress.gov/bill/99th-congress/house-bill/4311

the amphibole category. Instead, in serpentine asbestos, the fibres are curly in structure.

Chrysotile : Commonly referred to as 'white asbestos', this was used widely in commercial products due to its flexible malleability but also its heat-resistance and strength. It was therefore used extensively in roofs, as well as in walls and floors. It was also used to line vehicle brakes and as insulation.

(iii) Uses of asbestos

Of the six types of asbestos which are commonly identified, the three most commonly used commercially were; chrysotile, amosite and crocidolite. All three had good levels of heat-resistance, were flexible enough to be manipulated in shape and retained good core strength so as to be used for a variety of construction and manufacturing purposes. They were most notably used as insulation for fire-retardant safety products, and in a manufacturing context as linings for other manufactured products which would be exposed to heat, most notably; boiler linings, seals, and gaskets.

The use of asbestos was common particularly in the latter quarter of the 19th century and the first half of the 20th century due to the widespread use of mass production lines. However, its use pre-dates that period significantly. To demonstrate the widespread and varied use of asbestos, on 1st May 2011, The Guardian published an article[2] which opened with the line "Your home has a 50% chance of harbouring asbestos…". The risk of it being present lies everywhere from simple pipe lagging, to Artex ceiling coating.

In other contexts, there has been a noted issue in the United Kingdom in schools. In February 2012, the All-Party Parliamentary Group on Occupational Health and Safety had previously reported upon the widespread presence of asbestos in school buildings estimating that 75%

---

2 https://www.theguardian.com/money/2011/may/01/asbestos-hidden-health-hazard

of state schools likely contained asbestos[3]. In 2017 the Department for Education published a further report entitled 'Managing Asbestos in your School'[4] and then in 2018 commenced a further survey of schools which concluded in February 2019. Crucially, out of the DfE's survey, of those who did reply (some 2,952 schools), 2,570 confirmed that they believed that asbestos was present in at least one building on their premises. That is 87%, some 13% higher than that originally believed to be the case as per the 2012 All-Party report. A total of 676 schools failed to demonstrate any compliance or proper response and were reported to the HSE for investigation. On 10th March 2020, the National Education Union announced that the Joint Union Asbestos Committee ('JUAC') issued a statement of intent to further lobby government to spotlight the issue and to campaign for Regulations to enforce the safe removal of asbestos from schools by 2028[5].

Accordingly, given those two comparatively recent surveys which highlight the continued presence of asbestos in everyday life today, it can perhaps be better understood why the insurance industry continues to believe that the peak of asbestos-related industrial disease claims is yet to be reached as we outlined in our introductory chapter.

(iv) What makes asbestos dangerous?

Whilst this question will be discussed in more detail in the causation chapter, it is perhaps one to answer briefly early on in this text to assist understanding from the outset.

Essentially, when asbestos is disturbed, the individual fibres of asbestos become detached and are released into the atmosphere. This often manifests itself in dust, but in some cases, it can simply occur without

3 https://publications.parliament.uk/pa/cm201213/cmselect/cmeduc/writev/1056/m4.htm

4 https://www.gov.uk/government/publications/asbestos-management-in-schools--2

5 https://neu.org.uk/press-releases/joint-union-asbestos-committee-asbestos-crisis-our-schools

being seen and in total ignorance of it happening. If a fibre is inhaled or ingested by someone, then it can make its way into the lungs and internal respiratory system. The fibre can then become lodged in the tissue wall or lining of the lungs or windpipe and will settle within the tissue itself. The nature of the fibre is that it has a slow-burning, aggravated effect on the tissue which it becomes lodges in – asbestos is, accordingly, classified as a human carcinogen. Over time, the tissue becomes damaged by the reaction with the fibre and this can lead to inflammation and, eventually, the formation of tumours and other serious health conditions.

Though asbestos exposure which causes injury predominantly manifests itself in a variety of respiratory conditions, its potency is not limited to the lungs. Other cancers affecting non-respiratory organs can occur, though these are less common.

(v) Is asbestos still an issue today?

Asbestos regulation varies between states. Some have stricter rules than others. Some began to regulate sooner than others.

In May 2020, the Health and Safety Executive estimated that there were still around 5,000 asbestos-related deaths from exposure to asbestos at work[6]. That is despite it being prohibited to use asbestos in the construction of any building since 1999 – though crocidolite and amosite were both previously banned from 1985.

Consequently, there are a huge number of buildings which still, to this day, contain asbestos. In the construction industries where demolition of those old buildings occurs, potentially lethal exposure can still take place unless full precautions are taken.

The UK insurance industry is unsure when asbestos claims will peak, they still appear to be increasing in number year-on-year. It is estimated that the majority of cases will have come to light by 2028 but that is

6 https://www.hse.gov.uk/asbestos/dangerous.htm

always subject to change. The difficulty in being able to predict the number of cases principally arises from the difficulties in knowing that exposure has actually taken place, and the long latent period between that exposure and the onset of symptoms and subsequent diagnosis.

Of course, for those claims which are brought, their values can range significantly from being of a modest value for those whose exposure has resulted in injuries at the lower end of the scale, to very high-value claims for those with far more serious conditions and/or cases where the exposed person has succumbed to their asbestos-related injury and a claim is therefore advanced on behalf of their estate under the Fatal Accidents Act 1976.

In short though, and answering the question posed directly, asbestos is still a significant issue in the UK today and is likely to remain a significant issue for many years yet to come.

CHAPTER THREE
A BRIEF HISTORY OF MEDICAL AND INDUSTRIAL KNOWLEDGE OF ASBESTOS RISKS

Despite the widespread use of asbestos in the 19th Century, medical science was such that an understanding of a potential link between respiratory conditions and exposure to asbestos dust did not really begin to develop until the very end of that century.

The first warning was sounded in the Annual Report of the Chief Inspector for Factories and Workshops of 1898 in which the following passage was written:

> *"The evil effects of asbestos dust have also attracted my attention, a microscopic examination of this mineral dust which was made clearly revealed the sharp, glass-like jagged nature of the particles and where they are allowed to rise and to remain suspended in the air of a room, in any quantity, the effects have found to be injurious as might have been expected…"*[1]

The first substantive piece of research in relation to asbestos and its risks to health is generally attributed to that of William Cooke who wrote a piece in the British Medical Journal in 1924. William Cooke was a pathologist who had performed several autopsy's on patient's who had died at a relatively young age, from pulmonary fibrosis (a lung disease which causes extensive scarring to the inner lining of the lungs). In performing those autopsies, he noted the presence of asbestos fibres within the inner lung tissue and the presence of scarring around them. He termed the cause of death therefore as 'asbestosis'.

It should be stressed that other deaths had occurred where autopsies had revealed extensive presence of asbestos fibres within the inner lung

---

1 Page 172

tissues. However, it is generally William Cooke's article in 1924 which really focused the spotlight on asbestos and risks to health.

On the back of the article, the Government commissioned its then Chief Inspector of Factories, Edward Merewether and a Senior Engineer, Charles Price, to report on the status of the health of workers within the asbestos industry. That report[2] demonstrated that asbestosis was present in up to a third of those workers who were still working within the industry and that the presence was even higher (up to 80%) in those who had been working in the industry for over 20 years. The conclusion was that *'the inhalation of asbestos dust over a period of years results in the development of a serious type of fibrosis of the lungs.'*[3] It went on to say; *"It seems probable, therefore, although further research is very necessary, that not only is a certain minimal quantity of the dust required for the production of a generalised fibrosis, but that inhalation of the dust in high concentration results in the production of a more marked degree of fibrosis in a shorter time, than when the concentration is low."*[4] It was followed up by a further report by the same authors in 1931[5]. The guidance from the reports was to encourage the suppression of dust though further research into how that could be done was intimated to be required.

At that time though, it was thought that the issue was confined to the asbestos producing industry, and even then, only in those who had had a high level of exposure over a prolonged period of time.

In 1931 the Asbestos Industry Regulations consequently became enacted. They became effective in 1933 and sought to introduce control over exposure and to reduce it. Again, though focus was on high-level exposures which ought to be prevented by the suppression of dust and

2 'Report on the effects of asbestos on the lungs and dust suppression in the Asbestos Industry' by Merewether & Price published in 1930.

3 Page 9

4 Page 13

5 'Report on Conferences between Employers a& Inspectors concerning Methods for Suppressing Dust in Asbestos Textile Factories' by Merewether & Price published in 1931

the installation of ventilation to dilute concentration levels. The Regulations also required a degree of medical surveillance over works and, importantly, also made asbestosis a condition for which compensation could be claimed. There remained relatively little knowledge about other asbestos-related conditions which could also affect those exposed to asbestos dust.

In 1932 the Home Office investigated the risks of asbestos further and published their report 'Asbestosis-Inquiry into the Existence of the Disease in Packers of Manufactured Articles'. That report found: *"As a result of this enquiry we have formed the opinion that certain workers whose occupation is nominally that of packer, storekeeper or warehouseman, are exposed to a definite though very variable risk of contracting asbestosis."*[6]. That report indicated that the risks were prevalent to those not directly exposed to the dust in the course of their employment but who were exposed to background levels of dust of far lower concentrations.

There then came the Factories Act 1937, which prohibited, at section 47, exposure to *'any dust ...of such a character and to such an extent as to be likely to be injurious or offensive ... or of any substantial quantity of dust of any kind.'* The same, on its face, therefore include exposure to asbestos dust, though the phrase 'substantial quantity' was undefined. In 1939, the Annual Report of the Chief Inspector of Factories for 1938, discussed that section. The end comment read: *"It is not many years ago when the dust of asbestos was regarded as innocuous, while today it is recognised as highly dangerous."*

Despite Regulation, however, the use of asbestos continued in the UK and indeed, its use increased throughout the 2nd World War.

In the late 1940s Merewether again looked into the risks posed by asbestos in his 'Annual Report of the Chief Inspector of Factories for the year 1947'. He found that lung cancer had also been reported in 13.2% of cases of asbestosis that he had looked at. Further research was done by S.R. Gloyne in 1951 in which he found lung cancer present in

6 Page 4

14.1% of autopsies performed on those with asbestosis. In 1949 the Deputy Chief Inspector of Factories was referred to the issue of asbestos lagging in power stations and the application of the 1931 Regulations. The conclusion was:

> *"The Regulations do not apply to the removal of old lagging, nor to the actual application of the insulation to steam pipes etc. In regard to dusty processes which are outside the application of the Regulations, all possible steps should be taken against the inhalation of dust and the standards of the Regulations should be followed as far as practicable. Section 47 of the Factories Act 1937 requires that all practicable measures be taken to protect persons against the inhalation of inter alia, injurious dust and that when practicable, exhaust ventilation is to be provided. Apart from exhaust ventilation, other safeguards such as using suitable appliances for the operations, wearing respirators, avoiding unnecessary scattering and spillages and damping material before cleaning up, are of importance."*

By this time, the link between smoking and lung cancer had previously been made by Richard Doll in the early 1950s. The increasing presence of lung cancer in cases where an asbestos-worker had also developed asbestosis, however, began to be more closely monitored. Accordingly, in 1955 Doll published further research which looked, for the first time, at the presence of lung cancer in workers exposed to asbestos[7]. Doll concluded that *"The extent of the risk of lung cancer over the whole period among the men studied appears to have been of the order of 10 times that experienced by other men."*

At that point though, it was thought that the measures introduced in the 1931 Regulations had had a positive effective in reducing the numbers of asbestos-related injuries which had gone on to be suffered. It was believed to be too soon after their implementation to determine anything more in relation to future risks.

---

7 'Mortality from Lung Cancer in Asbestos Workers' published 1955 in the British Journal of Industrial Medicine: 485 – 490

In 1960 further research was, however, published by another group of pathologists J.C. Wagner, C.A. Sleggs, and P Marchand based on research commissioned in South Africa[8]. The research focused on 33 cases of mesothelioma (a malignant tumour of the pleura which had become more commonly seen in the Cape Province) of which it was made known that 28 had links to the Cape asbestos industry (either by direct employment or by their vicinity to mines) and where four of the other cases had involved men exposed to asbestos in other industries. Asbestos fibres were only found in 8 cases of those examined, though circumstantial evidence of exposure to asbestos dust was found in relation to the other cases. The paper is therefore widely credited as being the first to establish the link between mesothelioma and asbestos exposure – even on a low-level exposure basis and where exposure had not occurred during employment.

Accordingly, by the early 1960s, there were three known asbestos-related injuries; asbestosis, lung cancer, and mesothelioma.

At the same time, in the UK, the Ministry of Labour published an industry publication entitled 'Toxic Substances in Factory Atmospheres' which contained the first reference to exposure parameters to asbestos dust. In the 'normal working day' they specified that the Threshold Limit Value for Asbestos dust was 177 particles per cubic centimetre of air (ppcc) which translated to 5-30 fibres/ml. This was subsequently updated in 1966 and 1968 in respect to other substance exposures, but the threshold remained the same in each revision for asbestos.

In 1962, Wagnar published further research[9]. In 1964, W.G. Owen published a further paper on the link between asbestos exposure and mesothelioma picking up on the research by Wagner et al, and this time focusing on UK cases[10]. In his research, 17 cases of diffuse mesothe-

8 'Diffuse Pleural Mesothelioma and Asbestos Exposure in the North Western Cape Province' published in 1960 in the British Journal of Industrial Medicine: 260 – 271

9 'The Pathology of Asbestosis in South Africa' 1962

10 'Diffuse Mesothelioma and Exposure to Asbestos in the Merseyside Area' British Medical Journal 1964, 214 – 218

lioma were examined of which 14 cases had strong evidence of asbestos exposure, and exposure was suspected in the remaining. All told, the study covered both workers who had directly handled asbestos and others who had worked in clerical roles in offices which had a presence of asbestos dust. The study concluded that *"exposure to asbestos is a major factor, and possibly an essential one in the causation of diffuse mesothelioma"*[11]. Again, it was noted that the level of exposure to establish that causation, need not be high. Similar findings and conclusions were made by Elmes, McCaughy and Wade, through their research published in February 1965[12].

Also, in 1965, Newhouse and Thompson published more in-depth research into UK case of mesothelioma[13]. This time, 76 cases were examined, 23 of whom had direct asbestos exposure at work, 53 had no recorded exposure to asbestos, but 9 of those had second-hand exposure from people who worked at an asbestos factory and who they came into regular contact with, and another 11 worked within half a mile of an asbestos factory. This seminal paper concluded that mesothelioma could arise from even minimal second-hand and indirect exposure to asbestos dust and is regarded as something of a 'watershed' in industrial knowledge of low-dose exposure risks.

On 31st October 1965, soon after publication of Newhouse and Thompson's research paper, The Sunday Times published a headline article which discussed the research and the risks to health which flowed from exposure to asbestos. The article caused more widespread knowledge of asbestos risks beyond the industrial and medical sectors. Soon after, Mesothelioma caused by occupational exposure to asbestos became a prescribed industrial disease in August 1966.

A short time later, in December 1966, the Asbestosis Research Council published 'Recommended Code of Practice for Handling Asbestos

---

11 217

12 Diffuse Mesothelioma of the Pleura and Asbestos' British Medical Journal: 350 – 353

13 Mesothelioma of Pleura and Peritoneum Following Exposure to Asbestos in the London Area' British Journal of Industrial Medicine October 1965: 261 – 269

Products Used in Thermal Insulation'. That set out extensive guidance to the handling of asbestos in that industry, including; dampening procedures, the need for segregation when asbestos is cut or stripped, the use of protective sheeting within which dust should be collected and the installation of permanent or portable ventilation. Again, medical supervision and surveillance of workers was outlined.

On 3rd January 1968 The UK Medical Advisory Panel published research into crocidolite and highlighted its carcinogenic properties[14]. They recommend the exclusion of crocidolite wherever possible and called for greater controls to be more rigidly applied commenting that rapid expansion in volume and variety of asbestos usage had created problems in terms of the number of persons becoming exposed and the unsatisfactory working conditions which were persisting in parts of the industry. It was particularly noted that the potency of crocidolite was such that a safety level cannot be established or regulated.

Following on from that work, the British Occupational Hygiene Society published guidance on exposure parameters for chrysotile[15] and, for the first time, regulation began to differentiate between the different types of asbestos. Nonetheless, the report still referred to the risk posed by chrysotile dust as "small" and therefore set exposure limits which, in their view, *"could be tolerated for a lifetime without incurring undue risks."* and accordingly sought to reduce the risk of developing asbestosis to 1% by setting exposure parameters to chrysotile over 10, 25 and 50 year exposure periods.

The culmination of the research emerged during the latter half of the 1960s caused a review of the 1931 Regulations by HM Factories Inspectorate and eventually culminated in further regulation in the form of the 1969 Asbestos Regulations. Notably, the 1969 Regulations had far wider application than their predecessor. They set maximum exposure levels and applied to all work sites and not, as previously, to

14 'Problems arising from the use of asbestos: memorandum of the Senior Medical Inspector's Advisory Panel' 1967

15 'British Occupational Hygiene Society Hygiene Standards for Chrysotile Asbestos Dust' 1968

asbestos producing factories or facilities as before. They applied to all processes involving the use of asbestos and all items which were made up wholly or partly of asbestos[16]. These Regulations will be considered in more detail in Chapter 4, but Regulation 5 imposed strict obligations and requirements on employers and occupiers of premises where asbestos is used and all contractors on sites where asbestos was used or removed.

Accompanying the new Regulations was Technical Data Note 13[17] ('TDN 13') issued in early 1970 and which set exposure parameters as follows over a 4-hour weighted exposure period:

- Chrysotile & Amosite: 2 fibres/ml
- Crocidolite: 0.2 fibres/ml

These parameters were specifically for factory inspectors to determine whether exposure was *"to such an extent as is liable to cause danger to the health of employed persons"* under Regulation 2(3) of the 1969 Regulations.

From there, industry knowledge, led largely by government guidance, began to emit tighter and tighter restrictions with crocidolite ceasing to be imported from 1970 onwards.

In 1976 an Advisory Committee on Asbestos was set up by the Secretary of State for Employment. The aim of the Committee was to report on the risks posed by asbestos to workers and the general public, as well as risks from asbestos products and waste.

Also, in 1976, the Health and Safety Executive published Guidance Note EH10[18]. That maintained the exposure parameters which had been endorsed by Technical Note 13 but, crucially, and for the first time, gave the wide-ranging guidance that *"Exposure to all forms of*

---

16 Regulation 2(3)

17 'Standards for Asbestos Dust Concentration for Use with the Asbestos Regulations 1969' by Department of Employment and Productivity published 1970

18 Published December 1976

asbestos dust should be reduced to the minimum that is reasonably practicable."

In 1979 the Advisory Committee produced their final report. Their ultimate conclusion was that the control of useful but hazardous materials is preferable to prohibition of the substance. Prohibition was confirmed though in relation to the importation and manufacture of crocidolite products and to the application of asbestos material through spraying. The Committee encouraged the substitution of asbestos products wherever possible, and recommendations made to reduced exposure thresholds further to those specified in EH10 and TN13 previously and called for regulatory backing to reduce exposure to the 'lowest level reasonably practicable'. Increased medical supervision was also recommended to try and detect symptoms in workers as early as possible and to ensure that data could properly be obtained and recorded. PPE and effective ventilation in the workplace were also recommended.

In 1983, the HSE revised the 1976 EH10 Note in accordance with the recommendations in the Advisory Committee's final report. As such, they reduced the threshold exposure values taken over a weighted 4-hour exposure period:

- Chrysotile: 1 fibres/ml
- Amosite: 0.5 fibres/ml
- Crocidolite: 0.2 fibres/ml

In addition, further guidance was given to employers about how to reduce exposure to the 'lowest level reasonably practicable'.

In 1985, The Asbestos Prohibition Regulations 1985 came into effect which prohibited the importation and use of amosite and crocidolite. Likewise, it was also prohibited to supply products containing those materials under The Asbestos Products Safety Regulations 1985. Products containing chrysotile and amphibole asbestos remained widely available on the market however, but were required to be appropriately labelled. Following on then, in 1987, The Asbestos Products Safety

(Amended) Regulations 1987 came into force, and then later, in the same year, The Control of Asbestos at Work Regulations 1987. These latest Regulations were more ambitious and more substantive than their predecessors and required the total prevention of exposure to asbestos at work or to reduce the level of exposure to the lowest level reasonably practicable. These Regulations will be discussed in more detail in the preceding chapters.

More Regulation occurred over the coming years until, finally, in 1999 with the passing of The Asbestos (Prohibitions) (Amendment) Regulations, when chrysotile was also banned in the UK. Those regulations came into effect on 24th November 1999.

Following the prohibition on asbestos products being used in new products and installations, there has been further regulation, most notably The Control of Asbestos at Work Regulations 2002 and The Control of Asbestos Regulations 2006 – these will be discussed in more detail in subsequent chapters.

A highlighted version, for easier, and more fleeting reference, can be seen in the timeline at the conclusion of the Chapter.

It is hoped that that historical narrative provides a framework for some of the important medical, industrial, and indeed the regulatory developments which occurred from the late 1870s when the use of asbestos began to be commercialised.

1870s – Commercial Asbestos Sales Commence

1900 – First cases of Asbestosis noted

1924 – William Cooke article on asbestosis

1930 – Merewether & Price HM Factories Report

1931 – Asbestos Industry Regulations 1931

1937 – s47 of Factories Act 1937 comes into effect

1955 – Doll Research on asbestos exposure and lung cancer

1960 – Wagner et al on asbestos exposure and mesothelioma & Ministry of Labour's 'Toxic Substances in Factory Atmospheres' laying down the first exposure parameters for asbestos

1965 – Newhouse & Thompson paper on asbestos exposure and mesothelioma in the UK

1968 – UK Medical Advisory Panel report recommends ban on crocidolite

1968 – British Occupational Hygiene Society recommends exposure parameters for chrysotile

1969 – Asbestos Regulations 1969

1970 – Ministry of Labour Publishes TN13 setting exposure parameters for crocidolite, chrysotile and amosite

1976 – HSE published Guidance Note EH10 reducing exposure parameters to crocidolite, chrysotile and amosite or to *'lowest level reasonably practicable'*

1983 – EH10 revised and further reductions made to exposure parameters to crocidolite, chrysotile and amosite

1985 – The Asbestos Prohibition Regulations 1985 – bans crocidolite

1987 – The Control of Asbestos at Work Regulations 1987

1999 – The Asbestos (Prohibitions) (Amendment) Regulations 1999 – bans the use of asbestos in the UK

CHAPTER FOUR
THE DUTY OF CARE

The boundaries of where a Defendant's duty of care lies, has been a source of much debate in the Courts throughout the past four decades. In determining those issues, and establishing what the standard of care was, the Courts have had to delve into the historical overview of medical and industrial knowledge which we have just been through in the previous chapter. That history very much sets the scene and context of what was known to employers at a given point in time in the 20th century. As we have seen, regulation, or rather, effective regulation, came well after the evolution of scientific knowledge in respect of the risks posed by asbestos. Consequently, the common law has had to fill in the gaps for those employers who are alleged to have exposed their employees to asbestos prior to the 1980s when regulation really gained in momentum and breadth of application.

In the course of this chapter, therefore, we are going to split things into two parts. The first part of the chapter will look at how and where the Courts have set the details of the Defendant's duty of care, and the second will look at how that became more intricate following the introduction of regulation. Inevitably, of course, the content of regulatory duties, have been argued as matters which employers ought to have been aware of even before the regulations came on the scene, but of course there is a significant element of hindsight in that argument. It is for this reason that the detail of the medical and industrial literature on the issue has come under such scrutiny and is so important to understand.

In the context of the common law interpretation of the duty of care in asbestos claims, context really is the pinnacle issue.

PART ONE – THE COMMON LAW

(i) The Duty of Care

The classic exposition of an employer's duty of care is that of Swanwick J in Stokes v Guest Keen and Nettlefold (Nuts and Bolts) Limited [1968] 1 WLR 1776 at 1783:

> *"From these authorities I deduce the principles, that the overall test is still the conduct of the reasonable and prudent employer, taking positive thought for the safety of his workers in the light of what he knows or ought to know; where there is a recognised and general practice which has been followed for a substantial period in similar circumstances without mishap, he is entitled to follow it, unless in the light of common sense or newer knowledge it is clearly bad; but, where there is developing knowledge, he must keep reasonably abreast of it and not be too slow to apply it; and where he has in fact greater than average knowledge of the risks, he may be thereby obliged to take more than the average or standard precautions. He must weigh up the risk in terms of the likelihood of injury occurring and the potential consequences if it does; and he must balance against this the probable effectiveness of the precautions that can be taken to meet it and the expense and inconvenience they involve. If he is found to have fallen below the standard to be properly expected of a reasonable and prudent employer in these respects, he is negligent."*

That statement, was endorsed by Mustill J (as he then was) in Thompson v Smiths Shiprepairers (North Shields) Ltd [1984] QB 405, where he also added this:

> *'Between these two extremes [ie "without mishap" and "clearly bad"] is a type of risk which is regarded at any given time (although not necessarily later) as an inescapable feature of the industry. The employer is not liable for the consequences of such risks, although subsequent changes in social awareness, or improvements in knowledge and technology, may transfer the risk into the category of those against which the employer can and should take care.... In my judgment, this principle applies not only where the breach of duty is said to consist of*

> *a failure to take precautions known to be available as a means of combating a known danger, but also where the omission involves an absence of initiative in seeking out knowledge of facts which are not in themselves obvious. The employer must keep up to date, but the court must be slow to blame him for not ploughing a lone furrow.'*[1]

The phrase 'reasonably prudent employer' therefore begs the question of what such an employer would know of a risk and what they would then do to minimise it – the words 'knows or ought to have known' again are of particular importance. In short, the test removes the possibility of an employer relying on ignorance of a risk unless it was one which the 'reasonably prudent employer' would not have known of having regard to the wider knowledge which was generally available to employers during the period in question.

The starting point, therefore, is appreciation of the risk which then informs the crucial issue of foreseeability. A useful discussion of that issue is found in the following passage of the judgment of Simon J in Asmussen v Filtrona United Kingdom Limited [2011] 2 All ER 42:

> *"...the foreseeability of injury has to be tested against the standard of the well-informed employer who keeps abreast of the developing knowledge and applies [its] understanding without delay, and not by the standard of omniscient hindsight. The employer can rely upon a recognised and established practice to exonerate itself from liability in negligence for failing to take precautionary steps unless (a) the practice is clearly bad practice, or (b) in the light of developing knowledge about the risks involved in some location or operation a particular [University] acquired greater than average knowledge of the risks"*

Again, the passage emphasises the importance of considering what knowledge was available to a Defendant during the period in question. Accordingly, the knowledge has to be contextualised by what was available at that time and cannot be informed by knowledge gained

1 P415-6

after the event when hindsight can allow for different, and unfair, perspectives to be taken.

Accordingly, as will be seen from the following journey through the various cases, the disputes between parties have often resolved around the issue of foreseeability and in particularly what an employer could have reasonably have believed to have been a 'safe level' of exposure to asbestos dust in the sense that injury was not reasonably foreseeable below that level of exposure. The second, aspect to the case law is then the extent to which the duty is to apply against non-employees, or those victims not directly exposed during their work, but nonetheless exposed through coming into contact with employees who have been exposed at work, or as a result of workplace emissions of asbestos dust from factories.

(ii) **Large exposure cases**

It is probably best to begin by focusing on those more 'straightforward' claims – at least from a breach of duty perspective – where the Claimant can demonstrate regular, high-dose, exposure to asbestos. These are for Claimant's who worked with asbestos on a daily basis, or nearly daily, over a prolonged period of time, and so are the type of worker identified at risk in the very early medical literature emerging at the end of the 19th and beginning of the 20th century.

One such example are the joined cases of Jeromson v Shell Tankers (UK) Limited & Dawson v Cherry Tree Machine Co Limited [2001] All ER 24. The case involved claims brought by the estates of two former marine engineers who had worked for the Defendants in the engineer rooms of various ships between 1950 – 1957 and 1957 – 1961 respectively. Mr Dawson has also gone on to work for Cherry Tree and been exposed to asbestos there. Both had contracted mesothelioma.

When working for Shell, part of their duties involved stripping asbestos lagging from pipes within the engine rooms and in the process they said that they were exposed, without protection, to asbestos dust as a consequence. The exposure was therefore intermittent and, to some extent, limited but was nonetheless frequent. The issue, identified by Hale LJ, as she then was, was put thus:

> *"whether the degree of exposure in this case was such that a reasonable employer should have identified risk."*[2]

Just focusing on the Shell decision for present purposes, the Defendant argued that during the 1950s it was only realised that asbestosis could result from prolonged asbestos exposure over many years at a significant level – reliance for which stemmed from the Merewether and Price 1930 & 1931 publications. Mesothelioma, the condition from which both employees had passed away, was not linked to asbestos until 1960 and the exposure required to cause that was not known until after that date. Accordingly, the intermittent nature of the exposure in this instance, was argued to be of a different nature to that which would have caused identification of a material risk by Shell.

The Claimant argued that what was known was the dust to which these Claimants were exposed could be highly dangerous. No safe level was known and that accordingly, an employer could not simply sit back and say that no risk was foreseeable. At first instance the Judge accepted this submission and found for the Claimants. Hale LJ, thought likewise:

> *"The fact that other and graver risks emerged later does not detract from the power of what was already known, particularly as it affected employees such as these, working in confined spaces containing a great deal of asbestos which might have to be disturbed at any time. There is no reassurance to be found in the literature that the level of exposure found by the judge in this case was safe and much to suggest that it might well not be so. The judge was entitled to conclude that a prudent employer would have taken precautions or at the very least made inquiries about what precautions, if any, they should take."*[3]

2 Para 35

3 Para 52

Accordingly, it was held that further advice and thought, ought to have been given and that even for such intermittent exposure as in this case was found to have occurred, a respirator ought to have been supplied.

That is a somewhat classical application of the law in cases where exposure is more frequent and regular. In such cases, breach is going to be very difficult to defend if the Claimant proves their exposure on the facts.

(iii) The 'Safe Level' Debate – Low exposure claims

More problematic are cases where exposure is proved to be low-level or intermittent in the workplace. In such cases, many Defendant's rely on the literature which emerged in industry during the 1960s as being indicative – or at least, capable of being relied upon by the reasonably prudent employer – of safe and unsafe levels of exposure. Front and centre of this debate therefore is the Ministry of Labour's 1960 publication 'Toxic Substances in Factory Atmospheres' TN13 and the Health and Safety Executive's EH10.

Claimant's by contrast, have argued that the words 'safe limit' were never expressed in the documents and that therefore regardless of what exposure 'limits' were specified in that literature, the medical and scientific knowledge of the time made it clear that any exposure posed a reasonably foreseeable risk of injury and therefore ought not to have occurred without appropriate PPE.

Before looking at the caselaw, it is worth taking a closer look at what the Ministry of Labour's 1960 Booklet 'Toxic Substances in Factory Atmospheres' and particularly, its Preface, which contained the following statement:

> *"The threshold limit values refer to air-borne concentrations of substances and represent conditions under which it is believed that nearly all workers may be repeatedly exposed, day after day, without adverse effect. Because of wide variation in individual susceptibility, exposure of an occasional individual at or even below the threshold limit may*

> *not prevent discomfort, aggravation of a pre-existing condition, or occupational illness."*

Following that, the Booklet then set some exposure parameters for asbestos generally. Having regard to the first sentence of the preface, one can readily see how each side's argument would be put.

The issue of 'safe level' is particularly relevant in cases of low-level or isolated exposure to asbestos dust. Such an example was Williams v University of Birmingham [2011] EWCA Civ 1241. In that case, the Claimant had been a student at the Defendant's campus between 1970 – 1974. He recalled being exposed to asbestos dust from pipe lagging which was in disrepair for a period of around 52-78 hours. His exposure was found to be in the bracket of 0.1 fibre/ml – 0.2 fibres/ml. The Claimant passed away of mesothelioma in 2007 and his estate pursued the claim thereafter. The Defendant argued that they were, at that time, entitled to rely on the threshold guidance given in TN13 and that since, the Claimant's exposure level estimation did not exceed this, there was no foreseeable risk and as such, there could be no liability.

At first instance, the Defendant lost. The Judge determined that the exposure to asbestos had 'materially increased the risk' of the Claimant contracting mesothelioma, and that the Defendant knew, or ought to have known, that such low-level exposure could cause mesothelioma. As such a breach of duty was established. The Defendant appealed.

The Defendant argued that the Judge had applied the wrong test on the issue of breach of duty. The correct test was one of reasonable foreseeability as per *Stokes* et al, and not whether or not the Defendant had materially increased the risk that the Claimant would sustain injury – which was a test for causation.

In determining the issues under appeal, Lord Justice Aikens outlined the following overview of the steps which the Claimant needed to prove to establish his claim:

> *"...the claimant must show, first, that the defendant owed the victim a duty of care not unreasonably to expose him to asbestos fibres and*

> *the consequent risk of asbestos related injury, including mesothelioma. Secondly, the claimant must show that the defendant was in breach of that duty by being negligent in exposing the victim to asbestos fibres and consequent asbestos related injury that was the reasonably foreseeable result of that negligence. Thirdly, the claimant must prove, on a balance of probabilities, that the defendant's negligent breach of duty caused a material increase in the risk that the victim would develop mesothelioma. Lastly, the claimant must prove the loss and damage suffered in consequence of the injury and that it is within the usual "remoteness" rules."*[4]

In discussing the second element which was one aspect of the Defendant's appeal (others related to causation), the issue was encapsulated thus:

> *"...how does a court approach the issue of whether the defendant was in breach of that duty? The answer must be comparing what steps the defendant took to prevent the victim from being exposed to asbestos fibres with an objective standard of what reasonable steps should have been taken to avoid reasonably foreseeable injury in the factual circumstances prevailing at the time. The "reasonably foreseeable injury" in this case must be that of contracting mesothelioma."*[5]

The Court accepted that the trial judge had applied the wrong test for breach of duty. However, having regard to the levels of exposure found and the poor condition of the lagging in question which caused that exposure, the correct test could still be applied in the context of knowledge as it was in and around 1974. To that end, TN13 was highly relevant and Aikens LJ held as follows:

> *"In my view the best guide to what, in 1974, was an acceptable and what was an unacceptable level of exposure to asbestos generally is that given in the Factory Inspectorate's "Technical Data Note 13" of March 1970, in particular the guidance given about crocidolite. The University was entitled to rely on recognised and established*

4 Para 31

5 Para 32

> *guidelines such as those in Note 13. It is telling that none of the medical or occupational hygiene experts concluded that, at the level of exposure to asbestos fibres actually found by the judge, the University ought reasonably to have foreseen that Mr Williams would be exposed to an unacceptable risk of asbestos related injury."*[6]

As such, the Defendant's appeal was allowed and the finding of breach of duty was overturned. Curiously, there was no reference to the discussions in *Jeromson* or *Maguire* at all, in *Williams*.

Williams was followed by Mr Justice Bean in a subsequent decision in Hill v John Barnsley & Son Limited [2013] EWHC 250 (QB). That case which also centred on the degree to which an employer could rely on the exposure parameters in TN13 and the degree to which exposures to levels below those thresholds gave rise to a foreseeable risk of injury. Likewise, in McGregor v Genco (FC) Limited [2014] EWHC 1376 (QB), the Claimant alleged isolated exposure to asbestos dust in the mid-1970s when some escalators within a Department store, where she worked for the Defendant, were replaced. It was found to be unlikely that exposure parameters exceeded those in TN13. The Judge again found the exposure to be too small to put the Defendant on notice that the Claimant was at a foreseeable risk of injury.

TN13 again came under scrutiny in Woodward v Secretary of State [2015] EWHC 3604 (QB). Exposure to asbestos dust was alleged between 1976 – 1977. In respect of TN13, HHJ Platts (sitting as a High Court Judge), held:

> *"The risk of mesothelioma was known when TDN13 was published and it must be assumed that the health and safety executive knew of it when it was published. Notwithstanding that risk, it chose to set the exposure limits as it did. In effect, it seems what the HSE was saying was that exposure less than those limits was an acceptable risk and in my judgment any reasonable employer would be acting reasonably in accepting and following that guidance"*[7]

6 Para 61

7 Para 73

EH10 then came to be similarly considered in McCarthy (Executor of the Estate of Heward deceased) & Another v Marks & Spencer PLC [2014] EWHC 3183 (QB) in relation to sporadic exposure alleged to have occurred between 1976 – 1984. The Claimant alleged that, by this time, the Defendant's duty, in compliance with EH10 was to reduce the risk 'so far as was reasonably practicable'. At trial, the Judge found that the Claimant's exposure was below TN13 levels, in respect of EH10, he said:

> *"The experts are agreed that the levels of asbestos dust that the deceased would have been exposed to, whilst surveying and inspecting the ceiling voids, would have been less than the hygiene or control limit in force at the relevant times. Again I have concluded that the phrase "so far as is reasonably practicable" contained in HSE EH 10 (1976) did not extend by the standards of the time to requiring protective respiratory equipment and clothing to be used whilst the deceased was carrying out inspections…*
>
> *The extent of the risk that the deceased faced where his probable exposure did not exceed exposures of in the order of 0.01 to 0.03 fibres/ml (eight hour TWA) was below the level at which protective respiratory equipment was required, or indeed, recommended at the time. The guidance in HSE GN 10 (1976), having set out the control limits, refers to the use of a respirator in relation to crocidolite "unless the concentration in the breathing zone of a worker in a crocidolite process can be maintained below 0.2 fibres/ml when measured over any ten-minute sampling period." The significant factor is that the requirement only comes into play where the concentration of asbestos is above the control limit. There is no reference to the use of a respirator in relation to other types of asbestos."*[8]

As such, the Court held that the phrase 'so far as reasonably practicable' took a Claimant no further provided the exposure parameters of the time were not exceeded.

---

8 Paras 94-95

There then came something of a 'sea-change' in Bussey v 00654701 (formerly Anglia Heating Limited) [2018] EWCA Civ 243. The claim related to exposure between 1965 – 1968 when the Claimant worked for the Defendant and alleged that he would often have to cut through asbestos pipes when he repaired central heating systems and boilers. He developed mesothelioma in 2015 and subsequently passed away from the disease. At first instance HHJ Yelton (sitting as a Deputy High Court Judge) found exposure to be below the limits in TN13 and accordingly, following *Williams*, dismissed the claim. The Claimant appealed to the Court of Appeal on the basis that *Williams* was either wrongly decided, or ought to be distinguished and sought to argue that the TN13 parameters where not setting 'safe' and 'unsafe' levels of exposure but merely informed the parameters of enforcement which the HSE would look to under the 1969 Regulations. As such, the issues of foreseeability and breach were again thrown into the spotlight.

As a preliminary matter, the Court of Appeal rejected the Claimant's attack on *Williams* being wrongly decided. However, in discussing TN13, the Court 'clarified' what Aikens LJ was deciding. Lord Justice Jackson said:

> *"As previously noted, in [61] Aikens LJ held that TDN13 was the best guide to what were acceptable and unacceptable levels of exposure in 1974. He was not there formulating a principle of law. He was setting out a mixed finding of fact and law. That finding was based upon the expert evidence adduced in the case before him."*[9]

What was not correct however, was any interpretation that *Williams* stood for a rule of law that exposure below the TN13 thresholds was unactionable. On that aspect, Lord Justice Jackson went on:

> *"In my view TDN13 does not establish a 'bright line' to be applied in all cases arising out of the period 1970 to 1976. Still less is it a bright line to be applied to asbestos exposure in a different period whether before or after 1970 to 1974.*

9 Para 46

At this point in the analysis I regard it as relevant that neither Jeromson nor Maguire was cited in Williams. If Aikens LJ had those two decisions in mind, I do not think that he would have suggested (if indeed he did suggest) that TDN13 was a general yardstick for determining the foreseeability issue.

A more nuanced approach is required than that. It is necessary to look at the information which a reasonable employer in the defendant's position at the relevant time should have acquired and then to determine what risks such an employer should have foreseen.

I hasten to say that I am not criticising the actual decision in Williams. The deceased in that case was exposed to very low levels of asbestos for a relatively short time. The total exposure in Williams was much lower than the total exposure in the present case. The Court of Appeal very properly took into account the provisions of TDN13 in addition to the expert evidence.

I am not, therefore disputing any of the legal principles stated in Williams. Nor am I questioning the actual decision reached. The only gloss which, respectfully, I would place on the Williams judgment is this: Paragraph 61 should not be read as making TDN13 a universal test of foreseeability in mesothelioma cases."[10]

In *Bussey* itself, the level of exposure to which the Claimant had been exposed was just below the TN13 levels – though of course, at that time, TN13 was not yet published. The trial judge had found that there were ways of reducing that risk which the Defendant could have alerted the Claimant to. Putting that into the context of what was known at the time, Jackson LJ concluded:

"As things stood in 1965 to 1968 Anglia could not know, one way or the other, whether the extent of Mr Bussey's exposure was liable to cause mesothelioma. It might or might not do so. There were ready means of reducing that risk. In my view, if the judge had not felt constrained by the decision in Williams, he might have concluded

10 Paras 47-51

> *that, as a reasonably prudent employer, Anglia ought to have foreseen that risk; since that risk could be avoided by simple precautions, it was not a risk which ought to be accepted."*[11]

Lord Justice Underhill also weighed in on the argument:

> *"In particular, I think that the Judge was wrong to treat this Court in Williams as having laid down a binding proposition that employers were entitled to regard exposure at levels below those identified in TDN 13 as "safe", even in the period 1970-1976, still less at a period prior to its publication. There is the further point that in the present case, and I suspect in many others, there is no reason to suppose that the employer took any steps to measure the level of exposure which Mr Bussey or others doing similar work encountered and could not have accordingly known whether it was above or below any supposed "maximum safe limit". Attempting to answer the issue in this case by comparing back-calculations (it might be fairer to say "back-guestimations") of Mr Bussey's exposure against subsequently published figures of the kind appearing in TDN 13 is in my view unsound."*[12]

Accordingly, it ought to be appreciated that *Bussey* threw the 'safe limit' debate back into turmoil from a seemingly relatively settled state which existed in the years after *Williams.* TDN 13 was no longer the yardstick against which breach could be determined on the facts – in each case – that is so to cases concerning exposure before TDN13 came into being, and since.

There now seems to be a requirement for a Defendant, if it is to defend a claim on breach, to demonstrate evidence of what risk was appreciated and what steps were or were not taken in consequence of those risks – that comes most strikingly from Lord Justice Underhill's comments. In short, if a risk is identified (or ought to have been) but a Defendant leads no evidence as to what they did to try and reduce that risk – or at least assess whether or not they could reduce it – then they risk a

---

11 Para 57

12 Para 62

finding of liability even where the extent of the exposure is far below the TN13 thresholds.

In cases pre-TDN13, the Court of Appeal has re-affirmed the position which Lady Justice Hale had adopted in *Jeromson*, namely; where exposure parameters where uncertain, then the risk ought to have been considered by the Defendant in the context of the maximum likely level of exposure. Where that maximum level is below the subsequently published TDN13 levels, it does not mean that the Defendant will necessarily avoid liability – it depends on what the Court determines the reasonably prudent employer with knowledge of that maximum exposure, in the settings in which it occurred, would have done to minimise risk. It will then be over to the Defendant to demonstrate whether they properly took appropriate action in those circumstances. It also seems, from the judgment in *Bussey*, that the same approach applies to occupiers as well as employers.

(iv) Secondary Exposure claims

(a) Neighbourhood Claims

This category of claims relates to those not directly exposed by their employer but who nonetheless go onto develop an asbestos-related injury as a result of exposure in one of two circumstances; the first is where they live in close proximity to an asbestos factory and inhale dust thrown into the atmosphere by the work processes within, and the second is from familial members who have come into contact with asbestos dust as a result of being in close contact with employees who had been exposed at work. The most typical example of that latter category is a housewife who would wash her husband's work overall's which were contaminated with asbestos dust.

Beginning with that first category – those who lived closed to asbestos factories, a critical decision is that in the joint appeals of Margereson & Hancock v J.W. Roberts Limited [1996] PIQR 154. That concerned the Defendant's factory which produced products containing asbestos in the Armley district of Leeds. The Claimants were both local residents to the factory whose homes were within a few hundred yards. Neither Claimant had ever worked at the factory itself but one of the Claimants had been on the Defendant's site as a child and reported having played in bales of asbestos stored in their yard. Both Claimants went on to develop mesothelioma. Both claimed that their conditions were due to asbestos dust which the Defendant had negligently allowed to be released from their premises into the atmosphere. They alternatively alleged that a nuisance had been created. It was not in dispute that a substantial amount of blue asbestos dust had emanated from the factory and into the nearby atmosphere. At first instance, Holland J found for the Claimants. The Defendant appealed to the Court of Appeal.

The Court of Appeal determined that the issue was as per *Page v Smith*[13] in respect of foreseeability, but the Court clarified that in addition:

> *"...liability only attaches to these Defendants if the evidence demonstrated that they should reasonably have foreseen a risk of some pulmonary injury, not necessarily mesothelioma."*[14]

Debate stemmed around the date of knowledge of the risks posed by asbestos. The Defendant argued that knowledge could not be fixed prior to 1933, but this was rejected by the Court who held that there was an abundance of material, prior to that date, which made it clear that there were risks of pulmonary injury from the inhalation of asbestos dust.

The next issue focused on whether or not a difference in the duty applied between that owed to employees and neighbours. On that issue, the Court of Appeal agreed whole-heartedly with the findings of the trial judge:

> *"The final question to be posed and answered was whether any distinction could be sensibly drawn between employees working within the factory and the Plaintiffs involved in this litigation. As the Judge*

13 [1995] 1 AC 155

14 Per Russell LJ

> *put it "did the factory wall pose such a barrier that risk of injury to persons on the further side of such arising from the emissions of asbestos dust amount at worst to no more than 'a mere possibility which would never occur to the mind of a reasonable man'". The Judge said "there is nothing in the law that circumscribes the duty of care by reference to the factory wall ... if the evidence shows with respect to a person outside the factory that he or she was exposed to the knowledge of the Defendants, actual or constructive, to conditions in terms of dust emissions not materially different to those giving rise within the factory to a duty of care, then I can see no reason not to extend to that extramural neighbour a comparable duty of care". We agree. The Judge added "I have no doubt that in the immediate vicinity of the premises factory conditions in terms of dust emission were at various points effectively replicated so as to give rise to like foresight of potential injury to those exposed for prolonged periods"."*

Accordingly, the Claimants succeeded and effectively, the Court of Appeal outlined that the Defendant's duty was identical to neighbours in close proximity of their factories, as it was to their own employees, since from a foreseeability perspective, the same risks arose.

(b) Family member claims

In Maguire v Harland & Wolff PLC [2005] EWCA Civ 1 the Court of Appeal turned their attention to that second category of exposure where asbestos-related injury had been sustained by those who had come into contact with a family member whose work-clothes had been contaminated by asbestos dust.

In *Maguire*, the Claimant alleged that she had contracted mesothelioma as a result of washing her husband's work overalls which had been contaminated with asbestos dust from his work at the Defendant's shipyard between 1961 – 1965 as a Boiler Maker. The Defendant accepted that there was a reasonably foreseeable risk of injury to the Claimant's husband, but not to the Claimant. At first instance, the Claimant succeeded on liability. The Defendant appealed to the Court of Appeal.

The first instance decision was summarised thus at paragraph 17 of the decision of Lord Justice Judge:

> *"In summary, the essential question then posed by Morland J was whether it was fair to have expected Harland & Wolff to have addressed what we now know to have been the serious risk to the health of the wives of employees like Mr Maguire. "Was the risk to her and others in her position reasonably foreseeable in the period 1961-1965? If so, what steps could Harland & Wolff have been expected reasonably to have taken in that period?" He concluded, first, that the risk was indeed reasonably foreseeable and also that Harland & Wolff never considered or reflected on it, and, second, that elementary and simple precautions, such as changing rooms at work, and sensible showering and laundry arrangements, would have ensured that Mr Maguire returned home from work without wearing dust-infested clothing. Accordingly Harland & Wolff were liable to her."*

In the Court of Appeal, the Defendant argued that the risk to persons other than those directly exposed to asbestos in the course of their employment, was not known until Newhouse and Thompson's paper of 1965. As such, they argued that there was no foreseeable risk to injury in respect of secondary exposure victims, until after this date. The Claimant submitted that though that could be the case for the development of mesothelioma specifically, it was established prior to then that secondary exposed persons could be at risk of pulmonary injury and that was all that needed to be established and that the date from which that was established was 1960. That argument was based upon the Ministry of Labour's 1960 Booklet 'Toxic Substances in Factory Atmospheres' which contained the following reference:

> *"As some toxic materials can be absorbed through skin, exposed parts of the body should as far as practicable be covered by protective clothing. Contaminated clothing should be changed and hands, face and any other exposed parts of the body should be thoroughly washed at the end of the working day."*

The Court of Appeal considered the historical literature and a useful outline is given in paragraphs 23 – 42. The Court concluded that in terms of the test as to the extent of the Defendant's duty of care, the decision in *Margereson & Hancock* as to environmental contamination, was equally applicable to cases of familial exposure but that that was confined only to cases where the exposure of the family member was to the same extent as that which was present within the factory itself:

> *"The principle approved in Margereson and Hancock in relation to environmental exposure to asbestos dust has potential application to cases of familial exposure. In summary, a family member is not precluded from establishing liability based on environmental contamination with asbestos dust. In an appropriate case, the environmental principle may apply to members of an employee's family as to anyone else living in the immediate vicinity of premises working with asbestos. However, in this case, it was not established that the dust to which Mrs Maguire was exposed effectively replicated her husband's level of exposure, nor indeed that her level of exposure, if repeated in factory conditions, would have constituted a breach of duty to an employee. Therefore liability on the basis of "environmental" exposure did not arise for consideration."*[15]

This being a different type of case whereby exposure had been substantially less than the level within the factory itself, the Court of Appeal, looked at this category of exposure afresh. Commenting on the literature which they had surveyed, the Court said at 57:

> *"…until 1965, notwithstanding the increasing concerns and developing knowledge about the risks of exposure to asbestos among employees, nothing in the literature warned against the risks of familial or secondary exposure. On this topic, there was what appears to us now to have been a numbing silence. Before 1965 neither the industry generally, nor those responsible for safety and health, nor the Factory Inspectorate, nor the medical profession, suggested that it was necessary, or even that it would be prudent, for risks arising from familial exposure to be addressed by the industry. In truth, the alarm*

15 Per Lord Justice Judge at para 48

> *did not sound until late 1965, when it began to be appreciated that there could be no safe or permissible level of exposure, direct or indirect, to asbestos dust. Thereafter, the learning curve about the risks arising from familial exposure was fairly steep."*

Accordingly, the Court held that there was no foreseeability during the period in question in respect of Mrs Maguire. Lord Justice Longmore went on to add the following:

> *"If, therefore, one looks at the matter, as I think one should, from the perspective of the diligent managing director (or other safety officer) of a ship repairer such as Harland and Wolff in 1960-1965, who keeps up with the occupational literature, there is no indication that such a person ought to have appreciated the risk of exposure to asbestos dust on the part of those living in the same household as an asbestos worker or on the part of those laundering the employee's clothes. To so hold would be to use the hindsight of to-day to an unacceptable degree. It would also be to blame Harland and Wolff for not "ploughing a lone furrow" which, as Mustill J said in the industrial deafness case of Thompson v Smiths Shiprepairers [1984] QB 405 at 415B, an employer does not have to do.*
>
> *The courts should, in my view, be careful before they impose, in a scientifically developing field, standards which no employer ever thought of adopting at the time of the occurrence of the injury complained of. Exposure to asbestos dust is a classic case where knowledge and awareness of disease advances incrementally."*[16]

(v) Cases with Multiple Exposure Sources

This type of case occurs where a Claimant was exposed to asbestos by more than one employer/source and it is argued by one Defendant (or more) that in their employment, exposure was de minimis.

---

16 Paragraphs 94 – 95

Consideration of this type of case came before the Courts in Carey v Vauxhall Motors Limited [2019] EWHC 238 (QB). Between 1973 – 1979 the Claimant's husband worked for the Defendant as a maintenance electrician at their plant in Dunstable. He claimed that though he did not work directly with asbestos dust on a daily basis, his work overalls would often be contaminated with such dust and that he would then take his overalls home and give them to his wife to wash. Given the previous rulings in *Maguire* and *Magereson*, the Defendant admitted that their duty did not end at the factory wall and as such, that they owed Mrs Carey a duty of care and it was further admitted that by the time in question, they knew of the risks posed by exposure to asbestos dust to secondary exposure victims such as Mrs Carey. However, they argued that the level of exposure to Mrs Carey was minimal and accordingly denied that injury was foreseeable.

HHJ Yelton (sitting as a Deputy of the High Court) found that the exposure was more than de minimis and that as such a reasonably foreseeable risk of injury was present to both Mr and Mrs Carey. In reaching that conclusion, the Judge cited the decision of the Court of Appeal in *Bussey* as being the approach to follow in determining the issues of breach of duty – even in cases of secondary exposure such as the present:

> *"The Court has to consider whether Vauxhall fulfilled its duty of care by taking all reasonable care by taking all practicable measures to prevent Lydia Carey from inhaling asbestos dust, through contact with their employee John Carey, in light of the known risk that asbestos dust, if inhaled, might cause mesothelioma."*[17]

It will be noted immediately that is the 'nuanced approach' which was set out by Jackson LJ in *Bussey*.

In terms of the issue regarding the extent of the exposure, the Judge also cited the law on what was a 'material' contribution and particularly the

17 Paragraph 18

decision of Lord Reid in *Bonnington Castings Ltd v Wardlaw*[18] at page 621 where he had said:

> *"What is a material contribution must be a question of degree. A contribution which comes within the exception de minimis no curat lex is not material. I do not see how there can be something too large to come within the de minimis principle but yet too small to be material."*

In applying that decision, HHJ Yelton emphasised that determining whether exposure was more than de minimis was a fact-finding exercise which required a quantitative assessment based on both expert and witness testimony. It was noteworthy that no consideration of exposure levels as per TDN 13 were cited in *Carey* – the focus was entirely on whether the Defendant exposed Mrs Carey to a more than de minimis quantity of asbestos dose. The reasoning for that, is perhaps, that the Defendant conceded that they knew of the risks posed by asbestos by that time, combined with the effect of the decision in *Bussey*, but it's omission is curious nonetheless.

In short, though, *Carey* does make it clear that the exposure must be more than de minimis in order to be factored into the Court's assessment where is doubt raised by the Defendant that the culpable exposure came from another entity or source.

(vi) The boundaries between breach and causation

It is probably worth just finishing off with an issue which often arises in the context of asbestos claims; that is the common misconception that breach of duty is governed by the concept of 'material contribution to the risk of developing an asbestos-related' condition. It will often be seen that a Defendant denies breach of duty on the basis that the risk was unforeseeable or that the exposure to asbestos was, alternatively, de minimis or immaterial.

---

18 [1956] 1 AC 613

The temptation, therefore, is to view both as being arguments in defence of breach and that there are therefore two tests for breach. That was the error that the judge at first instance fell into in *Williams*.

In short, material contribution is a test for causation – as will be seen in the coming Chapter. When a Defendant alleges that the extent of exposure was de minimis or immaterial, in reality, they are saying no more than the exposure level was insufficient to give rise to a reasonably foreseeable risk of injury. A finding that the exposure was material – as occurred, for example, in *Carey* – is in effect a determination that there was a foreseeable risk arising from that level of exposure and that as such breach is prima facie capable of being imposed in the absence of adequate control measure being evidenced by the Defendant.

Accordingly, the two issues; breach and causation, need to be kept separately and the tests for both respects so as not to be interchangeably applied incorrectly in aspects of a case to which they do not, and should not apply. To do otherwise will lead to grave error.

(vii) Summary

The above discussion has therefore outlined how the issues of duty and breach have been determined in the common exposure categories of cases which often come before the courts. Plainly, different rules apply to different types of cases but the most relevant point to take away is that it is fact-sensitive to each case depending on the period over which exposure is alleged to have occurred.

It is doubtless the case that the decision in *Bussey* has significantly changed the landscape in that it marked a more fact-sensitive approach going forward with less reliance being available to Defendant's on retrospective estimations of exposure obtained in the course of the litigation as compared to threshold level maximums which were printed in government and industry guidance. Equally doubtless, is the fact that *Bussey* has made it more difficult for a Defendant to merely hide behind the burden of proof when it comes to the issue of breach of duty – rather there now appears to be more of a focus on not just establishing what the Defendant ought to have appreciated about the risk viz the Claimant, but also to demonstrate that something was done to minimise it, in order for a finding of breach to be avoided. Plainly, given the historical nature of asbestos claims due to the latency period in the injury caused, that is often going to be something which is difficult for a Defendant.

In short order, though, and bringing the above discussion together, the following principles now seem settled in determining breach of duty in cases brought in common law negligence:

- The starting point to is to assess what the reasonably prudent employer knew or ought to have known of the risks posed by asbestos.
- Second, that analysis then needs to be refined so as to specifically apply to the Claimant's alleged exposure which is informed by the nature of their relationship with the Defendant at the material time: i.e. large exposure, low exposure, secondary exposure etc.
- The Court must then ascertain whether, in those circumstances, the exposure was material so as to have made the potential for asbestos-related injury reasonably foreseeable. This is assessed again, by having regard to the degree of knowledge at the time.
- If the risk from exposure was material/foreseeable, the Court will then next seek to analyse what the Defendant did about the risk, as compared to what the reasonably prudent employer would have done at that time.
- Finally, the Court will assess whether, in light of the degree of risk, the extent of exposure, the knowledge of the Defendant, and the actions they took to minimise the risk to the Claimant, the Defendant did all that they reasonably could to ensure the safety of the Claimant.

PART TWO – STATUTORY AND REGULATORY DUTIES

(i) Introduction

As a result of Section 69 of the Enterprise and Regulatory Reform Act 2013, breach of health and safety regulations committed after 30 September 2013 will generally not be actionable as breach of statutory duty in civil proceedings, albeit an argument may be made by the Claimant that the statutory duty should inform the content of an employer's common law duty of care, or that breach of statutory duty should be taken to be evidence of negligence.

In the case of asbestos claims, where it is not unusual for the time between exposure and the manifestation of symptoms to have taken over 50 years, breach of statutory duty is of much more direct relevance as a cause of action because the alleged breach of statutory duty will have occurred when a breach of statutory duty was actionable in civil proceedings.

A number of statutory duties are typically employed in asbestos claims. These can be broken up into the following broad categories:-

- Statutory duties specifically designed to deal with asbestos.
- Statutory duties of general application which lend themselves to asbestos claims. Statutory duties designed for particular industries.

In each of these broad categories, however, the statutes and statutory instruments have been updated, consolidated and replaced over time. It is therefore important always to ensure, whether acting for the Claimant or Defendant, that the relevant statutory duties in force at the time in question are considered.

Below is a survey of the main statutory duties which are encountered in asbestos claims.

(ii) The categories of statutory duties

(a) Statutory duties specifically designed to deal with asbestos

The Asbestos Industry Regulations 1931 (in force, largely, from 1 March 1932 until 13 May 1970)

The first task is to analyse whether or not the case falls within "the Preamble" to the Regulations. This sets out the "processes" carried out in "factories and workshops or parts thereof" to which the Regulations applied, namely:-

> *"breaking, crushing, disintegrating, opening and grinding of asbestos, and the mixing or sieving of asbestos , and all processes involving manipulation of asbestos incidental thereto;*
>
> *all processes in the manufacture of asbestos textiles, including preparatory and finishing processes;*
>
> *the making of insulation slabs or sections, composed wholly or partly of asbestos, and processes incidental thereto;*
>
> *the making or repairing of insulating mattresses, composed wholly or partly of asbestos, and processes incidental thereto;*
>
> *sawing, grinding, turning, abrading and polishing, in the dry state, of articles composed wholly or partly of asbestos in the manufacture of such articles;*
>
> *the cleaning of any chambers, fixtures and appliances for the collection of asbestos dust produced in any of the foregoing processes".*

Although the Regulations refer to "the Asbestos Industry", the Supreme Court held in McDonald v. National Grid Electricity Transmission PLC [2015] AC 1128 ("McDonald") that the question was not whether or not the processes were part of "the asbestos industry", but fell within the wording of the preamble, upholding a view taken by the Court of

Appeal in Cherry Tree Machine Co Limited v. Dawson (Jeromson v. Shell Tankers (UK) Limited) [2001] ICR 1223.

The Preamble does, however, limit the application of the Regulations in some cases of sporadic exposure:-

> *"Provided that nothing in these Regulations shall apply to any factory or workshop or part thereof in which the process of mixing of asbestos or repair of insulating mattresses or any process specified in (v) or any cleaning of machinery or other plant used in connection with any such process, is carried on, so long as (a) such process or work is carried on occasionally only and no person is employed therein for more than eight hours in any week, and (b) no other process specified in the foregoing paragraphs is carried on".*

The Regulations are accordingly of broad application and address a number of processes. *McDonald* considered the meaning which should be given to "mixing" and determined that it should not be given a restricted meaning, and covered mixing asbestos powder with water in order to undertake lagging work.

The Regulations further applied to "occupiers". As *McDonald* itself illustrated, the person injured need not have been employed by the occupier, but could be any person who might be called upon to work in the factory in question, even if employed by another.

If the Regulations did apply, they imposed strict requirements for "exhaust draughts effected by mechanical means" to prevent the escape of dust into the air in which persons worked whilst undertaking certain processes (Regulation 1), and to suppress dust as far as practicable (during mixing or blending by hand) (Regulation 2). There were requirements as to the safe storage of loose asbestos (Regulation 4) and the construction and maintenance of machinery (in order to avoid the escape of asbestos) (Regulation 5). Regulations 6 and 7 imposed requirements as to cleanliness and safe methods of cleaning. There were, in Regulations 10 and 11, requirements as to personal protective equipment and, for certain processes, the use of breathing apparatus.

The Asbestos Regulations 1969 (in force from 14 May 1970 until 28 February 1988)

The next great "overhaul" of asbestos legislation was the Asbestos Regulations 1969, which revoked and replaced the Asbestos Industry Regulations 1931.

The definition of "asbestos dust" in Regulation 2(3) imported a requirement that the exposure be such as to be reasonably foreseeably harmful:- *"references in these Regulations to asbestos dust shall be taken to be references to dust consisting of or containing asbestos to such an extent as is liable to cause danger to the health of employed persons"*.

The Regulations were of general application, applying to *"every process involving asbestos or any article composed wholly or partly of asbestos, except a process in connection with which asbestos dust cannot be given off"*, and applying to the premises and places to which the Factories Act 1961 applied (including applying to building operations and works of engineering construction) (Regulation 3(1) and (2)). The Regulations, under Regulation 5, applied both to employers (in relation to its employers and premises, plant or material under its control) and occupiers of factories (in relation to certain provisions of the Regulations).

The Regulations required the use of exhaust ventilation equipment before processes involving asbestos were carried out (Regulation 7) and, if this was not practicable, the use of approved respiratory protective equipment and protective clothing (Regulation 8). There were also important and significant requirements to maintain a clean workplace and to clean by dustless methods (where practicable) (Regulations 9 and 10), relevant to claims where it is alleged that manual sweeping of asbestos waste was undertaken.

The Control of Asbestos at Work Regulations 1987 (in force from 1 March 1988 until 20 November 2002)

Most, but not all, claims involving asbestos exposure currently being litigated deal with exposure alleged to have occurred wholly, or substantially, prior to the entry into force of the 1987 Regulations. The

1987 Regulations carried forwards many of the protections of the 1969 Regulations but also significantly increased the regulation of asbestos in a number of respects, including the following:-

- A requirement under Regulation 5 to make an assessment of exposure in relation to any work which *"which exposes or is liable to exposure any of his employees to asbestos"*.

- A specific requirement under Regulation 7 to provide adequate information, instruction and training to employees.

- A general duty under Regulation 8 to prevent (altogether) the exposure of employees to asbestos, or, where that is not reasonably practicable, to reduce the exposure of employees to the lowest level reasonably practicable by measures other than the use of respiratory protective equipment (which were, accordingly, to be "the last line of defence", rather than "the first line of defence").

- The statutory introduction of the concept of "control limits" (concentrations of asbestos in the atmosphere) (both standard control limits, averaged over continuous 4-hour periods, and short-term control limits, averaged over continuous periods of 10 minutes, differing depending upon whether the asbestos in question was (a) crocidolite or amosite or (b) another type of asbestos). HM Factory Inspectorate (the predecessor to the Health and Safety Executive) had been using control limits as part of its regulatory functions since in or around 1970, as an aid to determine whether or not to take enforcement action – hence TDN13 and EH10 which we have already looked at. However, under the 1987 Regulations, if it was not reasonably practicable to reduce exposure to below all applicable "control limits", the provision and use of respiratory protective equipment, so as to bring exposure below the "control limits" was mandatory.

- There was a specific requirement under Regulation 15 to undertake, and record, air monitoring where "appropriate for the protection of health of" employees.

The Control of Asbestos at Work Regulations 2002 (in force from 21 November 2002 until 12 November 2006), the Control of Asbestos Regulations 2006 (in force from 13 November 2006 until 5 April 2012) and the Control of Asbestos Regulations 2012 (in force from 6 April 2012): the future

There is yet to be any reported personal injury / disease claim concerning these Regulations, due no doubt due in part to the long period of delay between exposure and illness which is typical of asbestos exposure claims (15 – 60 years from first exposure to the onset of disease being within the range encountered, with 35 years being average). It may also be due in part to the fact that (a) asbestos has, since the entry into force of the 2002 Regulations been better regulated than the 1960s and 1970s (which is the period of exposure still most commonly encountered in current asbestos claims) and (b) asbestos is significantly less commonly encountered now than it was in the 1960s and 1970s, when its use (both in terms of the manufacture and use of new asbestos products, and the remnants of old, existing products) was still widespread. In those circumstances, detailed consideration of those regulations is beyond the scope of this book. However, the period from 2002 saw rapid and substantial changes in the regulation of asbestos. The 2002 Regulations re-enacted and updated the 1987 Regulations, as well as imposing a free-standing duty to manage asbestos in non-domestic premises on the part of persons with responsibility to repair and maintain premises. There were extensions of the risk assessment and air monitoring requirements which the 1987 Regulations had introduced, as well as a duty on an employer to prepare specific procedures. The 2006 Regulations were designed both to strengthen and consolidate the existing protections against asbestos exposure.

The 2012 Regulations were introduced as a result of an investigation of the European Commission which determined that the 2006 Regulations had not fully implemented European Directive 2003/18/EC, which had the purpose of strengthening protection of workers from risks related to asbestos exposure. The 2012 Regulations largely replicated the 2006 Regulations but narrowed the types of work to which exemptions applied in relation to "low risk short duration work".

(b) Statutory duties of general application which lend themselves to asbestos claims.

The Factories Act 1937 (in force until 31 March 1962) and the Factories Act 1961 (in force from 1 April 1962 until, materially, the entry into force of the various "six pack" health and safety regulations made pursuant to the Health and Safety at Work etc. Act 1974 in the 1990s) are both statutory instruments with general application to asbestos claims without stating as much on their face.

The Factories Acts 1937 or 1961 (depending when the alleged exposure occurred) are widely used in asbestos claims because they contain specific requirements as to dust exposure and the safety and ventilation of workplaces. Due to the construction which the Court has given to some key provisions, the protection offered by those Acts in places mirrors the common law, but is, in places, potentially wider than at common law. Some of the main provisions (but not all) are addressed below.

Section 47 of the 1937 Act and Section 63 of the 1961 Act

Under Section 63 of the 1961 Act:

> *"in every factory in which, in connection with any process carried on, there is given off any dust or fume or other impurity of such a character and to such extent as to be likely to be injurious or offensive to the persons employed, or any substantial quantity of dust of any kind, all practicable measures shall be taken to protect the persons employed against inhalation of the dust or fume or other impurity and to prevent its accumulating in any workroom, and in particular, where the nature of the process makes it practicable, exhaust appliances shall be provided and maintained, as near as possible to the point of origin*

of the dust or fume or other impurity, so as to prevent its entering the air of any workroom".

Section 47 of the 1937 Act is identically worded.

The effect of these sections came to be discussed in the House of Lords. Per Lord Kerr SCJ at paragraph 87 of McDonald v. National Grid Electricity Transmission PLC [2015] AC 1128 ("McDonald"):

"proper application of the subsection requires a staged approach: (i) is the dust, fume or other impurity which is given off of such a character and given off to such an extent as to be likely to be injurious or offensive to the persons employed? (ii) if not, has any substantial quantity of dust of any kind been given off in the workroom where the Claimant was a person employed? (iii) if the answer to (i) or (ii) is "yes" are there practicable measures which can be taken to protect the persons employed against inhalation of the dust or fume or other impurity and to prevent its accumulation in any workroom? And (iv) if the answer to (iii) is "yes" have they been taken?".

As to whether dust is "likely to be injurious", as Pearson J, as he then was, stated in Richards v. Highway Ironfounders (West Bromwich) Limited [1957] 1 WLR 781 ("Richards") at 782 – 783[19]:

"Therefore, the phrase "likely to be injurious or offensive to the persons employed" has been interpreted, in what may be called a subjective sense, as meaning likely to be injurious or offensive according to the estimation of a reasonably well-informed factory occupier, or which the actual occupier knew or ought to have known to be likely to be injurious or offensive". Accordingly, to be "injurious", the dust must have been reasonably foreseeably hazardous by reference to the standards of the time.

However, whether or not "any substantial quantity of dust of any kind been given off in the workroom where the Claimant was a person employed" is a different question. "The question whether the

19 Para 86

> *dust is asbestos or other injurious dust should therefore not obtrude into the initial assessment of whether the second limb of section 47(1) is engaged" (paragraph 87). "The duty to take all practicable measures is triggered when there is given off any injurious or offensive dust or fume or any substantial quantity of dust of any kind. The subsection does not stipulate that the quantity of dust must be substantial at the point of inhalation" (paragraph 73). Whether or not there was a substantial quantity of dust "calls for a purely quantitative assessment".*

That assessment *"is a factual question for the trial judge dependant on the evidence in the particular case"* as per Prater v. British Motor Holdings Limited Unreported County Court, 9/6/2016, per Mr. Recorder Christopher Gardner QC, at paragraph 11.

Further, as Mr. Peter Marquand, sitting as a Deputy High Court Judge, said at paragraph 54 of Hawkes v. Warmex Limited [2018] EWHC 205 (QB) ("Hawkes"): "Substantial" has been interpreted as meaning "lots of dust" and more recently "a considerable quantity of dust" and the point at which the assessment of that should be undertaken is when the dust is produced, not when it is inhaled. In Ebbs v James Whitson & Co [1952] 2 QB 877 Bagnall J, considering section 63 of the Factories Act 1961 (the same wording as section 47 of the 1937 Act), stated: "'Substantial', in my view, does not mean merely 'not negligible': there must be, to use a common phrase, 'a lot of dust'; and it must be substantial when given off, not substantial merely by accumulation over a period."

Accordingly, due to *McDonald*, Section 37 / 63 are important provisions because if "substantial" dust is generated, it need not be "injurious" (e.g. reasonably foreseeable by reference to the standards of the time). Whether or not dust is "substantial" is, however, a factual question which can depend upon quite close analysis of the evidence on the subject.

Section 4 of the 1937 Act and Section 4 of the 1961 Act

Under Section 4 of the 1961 Act (with Section 4 of the 1937 Act being worded materially the same) *"effective and suitable provision shall be made for securing and maintaining by the circulation of fresh air in each workroom the adequate ventilation of the room, and for rendering harmless, so far as practicable, all such fumes, dust and other impurities generated in the course of any process or work carried on in the factory as may be injurious to health"*. This provision largely mirrors the common law, because "injurious to health" falls to be judged according to the standards of the time, in accordance with *Richards*, as set out above.

Section 26 of the 1937 Act and Section 29 of the 1961 Act

Under Section 29(1) of the 1961 Act *"there shall, so far as is reasonably practicable, be provided and maintained safe means of access to every place at which any person has at any time to work, and every such place shall, so far as is reasonably practicable, be made and kept safe for any person working there"*. Again, however, the view of the majority of the Supreme Court in Baker v. Quantum Clothing Group Limited [2011] 1 WLR 1003 was that *"safety must, in my view, be judged according to the general knowledge and standards of the times"* (paragraph 80, per Lord Mance JSC). Accordingly, in terms of the degree of risk which must be proven, these provisions mirror the common law. A potentially important difference, however, is that, if that degree of risk is proven, the burden is upon the Defendant to plead and prove that such care as was reasonably practicable was taken (as opposed to common law, where all burdens, evidential and legal, are upon the Claimant to show negligence).

The Occupiers' Liability Act 1957

At first sight, the "common duty of care" of an occupier to the visitor of premises under the Occupiers' Liability Act 1957 (the common duty of care is a duty to take such care as in all the circumstances of the case is reasonable to see that the visitor will be reasonably safe in using the premises for the purposes for which he is invited or permitted by the occupier to be there) might be thought to be of direct relevance. However, the Court of Appeal's decision in Fairchild v. Glenhaven

Funeral Services Limited [2002] 1 WLR 1052 means that the 1957 Act imposes liability arising from "the state of premises", rather from activities carried on at the premises by the occupier or third parties. To impose a duty of care in relation to activities carried on, either the common law or other statutory duties must be invoked:

> *"the statutory duty of care created by that Act imposed a duty on those occupiers to see that Mr Fairchild was reasonably safe in using the premises for the purposes for which he entered them, and he encountered no dangers in his use of the premises, as he would have done if he had fallen through an unguarded hole in the floor. It was what was going on in those premises which caused him harm"*

(c) Statutory duties designed for particular industries

There were various provisions for particular areas of industry, which broadly mirrored, so far as applicable, the requirements of the Factories Act. However, the following deserve brief mention, by way of example.

The Construction (General Provisions) Regulations 1961

Regulation 20 provided as follows:-

> *"20. Inhalation of dust and fumes to be prevented*
>
> *Where in connection with any grinding, cleaning, spraying or manipulation of any material, there is given off any dust or fume of such a character and to such extent as to be likely to be injurious to the health of persons employed all reasonably practicable measures shall be taken either by securing adequate ventilation or by the provision and use of suitable respirators or otherwise to prevent inhalation of such dust or fume".*

Under Regulation 2, the 1961 Regulations applied to "building operations" and, under Regulation 3: *"it shall be the duty of every contractor, and every employer of workmen, who is undertaking any of the operations or works to which these Regulations apply— (a) to comply with such of the requirements of the following Regulations as affect him or any workman employed by him, that is to say, ...*"

As addressed above in relation to the Factories Act, following *Richards*, the correct construction to be given to "likely to be injurious" is that dust had to be given off which was reasonably foreseeably hazardous by reference to the standards of the time.

The Shipbuilding and Ship-repairing Regulations 1960

Section 53 provided as follows:-

> *"Removal of dust or fumes*
>
> *53.—(1) Where in connection with any process carried on on board, in or on the outside of a vessel or part of a vessel there is given off any dust or fume or other impurity of such a character and to such extent as to be likely to be injurious to the persons employed, all practicable measures shall be taken to protect the persons employed against inhalation of the dust or fume or other impurity, and in particular, where practicable, exhaust appliances shall be provided and maintained, as near as possible to the point of origin of the dust or fume or other impurity, to protect such persons against such inhalation".*

Again, mirroring the protection found in the Factories Acts, following *Richards*, the correct construction to be given to "likely to be injurious" is that dust had to be given off which was reasonably foreseeably hazardous by reference to the standards of the time.

CHAPTER FIVE
BREACH OF DUTY & EVIDENCE

This next Chapter builds upon the last in that it aims to highlight some of the practical issues which will manifest themselves as each party looks to build their case on the fundamental issue of breach.

In dealing with this issue it must be borne in mind that, inevitably, in asbestos claims you will be dealing with events which have normally occurred decades prior to the date of trial. That passage of time will consequently cause inhibiting factors which will lead to difficulties, on both sides, in being able to effectively obtain reliable information, and effectively investigate lines of enquiry which emerge. More often than not, witnesses have passed away or are now untraceable, Defendant companies have been liquidated and require restoration, and documentation has, at best been destroyed, or at worst, there is uncertain as to whether or not it ever did exist.

We will look now at how each of these categories of evidence ought to be approached in the context of asbestos claims and look to give some practical guidance on how each can be most effectively used.

(i) Witness Evidence

Of course, witness evidence, from the Claimant's perspective, is always the bed rock of the claim. That is the case in most claims, but in claims of an historical nature it is often even more crucial since it is that statement which really sets all other investigations going and allows the lawyers to really try and get a feel for the all-important context of the claim which, as we have seen, is so important in asbestos cases, in evaluating the extent of the duty of care and whether or not there is a breach.

In asbestos-injury claims, because of the nature of the injuries which can ensue, and the fact that they can often develop – or indeed will have already developed – into terminal illness, means that the Claimant's testimony is best committed to paper at an early juncture. It will therefore often be done at or shortly after, the time when the Letter of Claim is first drafted, and it will normally be done in the absence of disclosure. That can cause problems later on down the line, as inevitably, there will be the temptation not to over-commit in the first statement with a view to reserving some positions so that they can be more fully set out at a later juncture when more evidence is available. That is, of course, a double-edged sword in cases where firstly, you are discussing events which go back many years and therefore the memory is already inhibited due to the passage of that time, and secondly, in cases where the Claimant's health is such that it could take a turn for the worse at any time.

The issues involving historical accounts being given by witnesses, has previously been highlighted by the Courts in other (non-asbestos) claims. Perhaps the most prominent and authoritative is Gestmin SPGS SA v Credit Suisse (UK) Limited [2013] EWHC 3560 (Comm) where Leggatt J stated:

> *"An obvious difficulty which affects allegations and oral evidence based on recollection of events which occurred several years ago is the unreliability of human memory.*
>
> *16. While everyone knows that memory is fallible, I do not believe that the legal system has sufficiently absorbed the lessons of a century of psychological research into the nature of memory and the unreliability of eyewitness testimony. One of the most important lessons of such research is that in everyday life we are not aware of the extent to which our own and other people's memories are unreliable and believe our memories to be more faithful than they are. Two common (and related) errors are to suppose: (1) that the stronger and more vivid is our feeling or experience of recollection, the more likely the recollection is to be accurate; and (2) that the more confident another*

person is in their recollection, the more likely their recollection is to be accurate.

...

19. The process of civil litigation itself subjects the memories of witnesses to powerful biases. The nature of litigation is such that witnesses often have a stake in a particular version of events. This is obvious where the witness is a party or has a tie of loyalty (such as an employment relationship) to a party to the proceedings. Other, more subtle influences include allegiances created by the process of preparing a witness statement and of coming to court to give evidence for one side in the dispute. A desire to assist, or least not to prejudice, the party who has called the witness or that party`s lawyers, as well as a natural desire to give a good impression in a public forum, can be significant motivating forces.

20. Considerable interference with memory is also introduced in civil litigation by the procedure of preparing for trial. A witness is asked to make a statement, often (as in the present case) when a long time has already elapsed since the relevant events. The statement is usually drafted for the witness by a lawyer who is inevitably conscious of the significance for the issues in the case of what the witness does nor does not say. ...The statement may go through several iterations before it is finalized. Then, usually months later, the witness will be asked to re-read his or her statement and review documents again before giving evidence in court. The effect of this process is to establish in the mind of the witness the matters recorded in his or her statement and the other written material, whether they be true or false, and to cause the witness`s memory of events to be based increasingly on this material and later interpretations of it rather than on the original experience of the events.

...

22. ... This does not mean that oral testimony serves no useful purpose ... But its value lies largely, as I see it, in the opportunity which cross-examination affords to subject the documentary record to

> *critical scrutiny and to gauge the personality, motivations and working practices of a witness, rather than in testimony of what the witness recalls of particular conversations and events. Above all, it is important to avoid the fallacy of supposing that, because a witness has confidence in his or her recollection and is honest, evidence based on that recollection provides any reliable guide to the truth."*[1]

Best practice accordingly dictates for a thorough 'proof' of the Claimant's evidence to be taken at an early stage with as much detail as possible outlined within. Of course, that proof is protected by privilege which allows for it to be obtained as a base from which other investigations can develop and a fuller statement taken once those investigations have been given an opportunity to progress.

Defendant's will often expect to see a statement from the Claimant at an early stage – around the same time as medical evidence is served, if not sooner. Whilst that can be to obtain a litigation advantage, more fundamentally the Defendant needs it to commence their own investigations since the insurance company or solicitor nominated on their behalf, will, at least initially, be dealing with matters without much primary documentation or material to go off and with a company which has long been dissolved and therefore with no immediately available witnesses to hand.

Any witness evidence which is obtained needs to be thorough, rational and consistent throughout. Inconsistencies can have a disastrous effect in historical claims as inevitably they call into question whether or not the witness is a reliable historian upon whose testimony the Court will be comfortable making findings of fact. As we have seen, in asbestos cases, they are each fact-sensitive on the issue of breach and the Courts analysis will therefore always start with findings on the nature and extent of exposure.

There are some good illustrations outlining the importance of witness evidence in asbestos cases. The first is *Carey*[2] which we have already dis-

1 Para 15 – 22

2 Ibid

cussed in the previous Chapter. In that case, the Claimant, Mrs Carey, had provided three witness statements prior to trial. She sadly passed away in the days leading up to trial and as such those witness statements, in their written form, had to stand as the entirety of her evidence. Though she had her husband's evidence to also progress the claim on, her evidence as to her exposure was limited to those statements. However, the quality of the statements were such that they were taken down to the last detail on the issue of how she would wash her husband's clothes – including the equipment, the technique and how that enabled fibres to be lifted from the overalls she was washing and be dispersed into the atmosphere in very close proximity to her. That is outlined in paragraph 26 of the judgment and is then ultimately the platform which enabled the Court to go on and make the favourable findings that it did.

Another example has more recently come before the High Court in Bannister v Freemans PLC [2020] EWHC 1256 (QB). This case concerned an isolated exposure allegation made by the Claimant stemming from events during his employment with the Defendant between 1977/78 – 1988/89. Mr Bannister had passed away from mesothelioma around a year prior to trial, the claim was continued by his estate. He alleged that, at some point during his employment, partition walls in his office had been removed by workmen over a weekend and that the walls contained asbestos. In the course of removing it, the asbestos was disturbed and asbestos dust consequently settled on his desk and surrounding area and cleaners had come in when he was at work and cleaned it up but in the process dispersed the dust into the atmosphere. The Claimant gave two witness statements in support of his claim and alleged that he knew the walls contained asbestos because a memo had been circulated prior to the work being done.

The Claimant had given his evidence by deposition prior to his death (something which shall be discussed in the Procedure Chapter). Both his statements and his performance when giving his evidence by deposition, were scrutinised by the Court and inconsistencies noted. The Court concluded:

"Firstly, although I accept, as did Mr Platt, that both the Deceased and Mr Ford did not give their evidence with any intention to deceive, there were a number of matters which made me have substantial doubt as whether the Deceased`s recollection of events could be relied upon. My reasons for so concluding may be summarised as follows.

Firstly, although I note what the Deceased said in cross examination, as set out above, namely that when asked about any exposure to asbestos he believed that the doctors were only interested in recent exposure and I accept Dr Moore-Gillon`s evidence that such denials of exposure to asbestos are not uncommon, such matters notwithstanding, it is in my judgment at the very least surprising that the Deceased denied being exposed to asbestos on three separate occasions during which time he would have had time to reflect on the accuracy of such denials.

Secondly, even after making substantial allowances for the fact that his cross-examination took place only 3 weeks before the Deceased died and that in my non-medical view he looked, and must have been, unwell when giving evidence on commission, I did not find what the Deceased said in his IIDB application form as to his alleged exposure to asbestos at all satisfactory…

Thirdly, even in his first witness statement the Deceased did not refer to the existence of the memo although he does refer to being told, in unspecified manner, that the following weekend workmen were to remove all partitions and of his belief that the partitions contained asbestos. Although the Deceased refers to the memo in his second witness statement and that the memo had highlighted the fact that the infill material around the partitions contained asbestos which was to be removed, I am satisfied that the Deceased had forgotten the existence of any memo until he was reminded thereof by Mr Ford.

Fourthly, there is a significant difference between the evidence of the Deceased and Mr Ford as to what parts of the partition were removed. The Deceased`s first witness statement said that on his

> *return to work on the Monday morning there were no partitions between the offices whereas in his second witness statement he stated that on the Monday, the steel frames of the partitions remained with some of the central pieces of the partitions removed but that there were gaps above and the sides of such partitions where the material used to fill such gaps. By contrast, Mr Ford's evidence, which was relied upon by the Claimant and which I accept, was that only the infill material at the edges of the partition were removed. So it is that the Claimant's case does not rely on that part of the Deceased's evidence which referred to the removal of the central pieces of the partition."*

That forensic critique of the Claimant's evidence properly underlines the need to have settled and reliable evidence which is consistent throughout – both with itself, and with the other documents which emerge in the course of the case. In *Bannister*, it made the difference between winning and losing as the Judge determined that the dust in question was probably not asbestos dust and that the Defendant had most likely brought in reputable contractors to dispose of any asbestos which had been present[3].

From a Defendant's perspective, identical considerations apply. Of course, a Defendant's evidence is slightly less specific in the majority of cases, since the chances of having a primary witness to the exposure events of which the Claimant makes complaint is relatively thin. However, the principles remain the same; detail is crucial and consistency – both with other witness accounts and with contemporaneous documents – is vital.

(ii) Documentary Evidence

Similar considerations must equally apply to documentary evidence. Where Defendants are dissolved many years after exposure occurred, there will inevitably be difficulties in identifying documentation of rel-

3 At the time of writing it is unknown whether the Claimant will try to appeal the decision – but nonetheless, the illustration remains valid for present purposes

evance. However, plainly, as can be seen from the cases which we have looked at, documentary evidence has a vital role to play when it is available.

Health and Safety documents which form some sort of risk assessment as to the nature of exposure to asbestos and precautions which are to be taken to minimise exposure risk, are the most pertinent of documents which need to be looked for. Of course, their provenance and reliability need to be cross-checked particularly when there is the risk that they contradict witness evidence which is also available. Ultimately, it must be remembered that the way something is written is not necessarily a proper reflection of the reality.

Categories of documentary evidence which are important to investigate are as follows:

- Health and Safety reports and memorandum
- Risk Assessments
- Dust surveys
- Evidence of health surveillance
- Personnel records
- Occupational Health records
- Evidence relating to the provision and supply of appropriate PPE

(iii) Inferences

In industrial disease claims generally, given the passage of time which has often elapsed between exposure and trial, inferences as to what was likely to have been the situation at the time, are often sought. This remains true particularly, in cases concerning asbestos exposure and then in relation to the issue of causation where there have been multiple sources of exposure or causative agents.

The issue of inferences inevitably comes from the interplay between different aspects of evidence on common issues and the Court's assessment of what is more likely to have occurred given the evidence which is available. An example is the decision in *Carey*, on the issue of whether or not the Defendant operated a compulsory scheme to wash work overalls so that employees did not have to take them home to be washed. The Defendant obtained a witness statement from the person in charge of the scheme at the Defendant but did not call him as a witness. As a consequence, at paragraph 29 of her judgment HHJ Walden-Smith found that the scheme had not been compulsory and that it was quite possible that the Claimant took his overalls home to be washed as he claimed.

However, the process of drawing inferences on the primary facts of exposure are issues which have been discussed in separate case law which it is important to adhere to. For Claimants, the allegation will often be that a Defendant has failed to call evidence on an issue and consequently an inference should be drawn in the Claimants favour. The most classic line of argument is Keefe v Isle of Man Steam Packet Co Limited [2010] EWCA Civ 683 and arises where a Claimant seeks to argue that a breach by a Defendant (such as performing a risk assessment or survey) has prevented the Claimant from proving his claim since evidence which ought to be available to him is now not. Consequently, the argument will be that the Defendant ought not benefit from their breach and that this can be protected by an inference of fact being drawn by the Court in the Claimant's favour. The argument was encapsulated in *Keefe* by Lord Justice Longmore at paragraph 19:

> *"If it is a defendant's duty to measure noise levels in places where his employees work and he does not do so, it hardly lies in his mouth to assert that the noise levels were not, in fact, excessive. In such circumstances the court should judge a claimant's evidence benevolently and the defendant's evidence critically. If a defendant fails to call witnesses at his disposal who could have evidence relevant to an issue in the case, that defendant runs the risk of relevant adverse findings see British Railways Board v Herrington [1972] AC 877, 930G. Similarly a defendant who has, in breach of duty, made it difficult or*

> *impossible for a claimant to adduce relevant evidence must run the risk of adverse factual findings. To my mind this is just such a case."*

Keefe itself, was a noise-induced hearing loss claim, however, its general application is obvious.

Defendants will argue for a more cautious fact-sensitive approach and will need to offer some explanation for the absence of evidence so as to prevent an inference being drawn against them.

The issue recently came before the Court of Appeal in MacKenzie v Alcoa Manufacturing (GB) Limited [2019] EWCA Civ 2110. *Keefe* was expressly considered and examined by the Court, as was a plethora of other case law relevant to the issue of inferences. Giving the lead judgment of the Court, Lord Justice Dingemans held:

> *"It seems therefore that it is possible to state the following propositions: First, whether it is appropriate to draw an adverse inference, and if it is appropriate to draw an inference, the nature and extent of the inference, will depend on the facts of the particular case, see Shawe-Lincoln at paragraphs 81-81. Secondly, silence or a failure to adduce relevant documents may convert evidence on the other side into proof, but that may depend on the explanation given for the absence of the witness or document, see Herrington at page 970G, Keefe at paragraph 19 and Petrodel at paragraph 44."*

A useful illustration of inferences in the context of an asbestos claim is Wilmore v Knowlsey Metropolitan Borough Council [2009] EWHC 1831 (QB). The case concerned alleged exposure to asbestos in one of the Defendant's schools between 1972 – 1979 from which the Claimant had sustained mesothelioma. The Claimant had been a pupil at the time of alleged exposure and alleged she had been exposed to various works which had taken place on ceiling tiles which contained asbestos. Mr Justice Nicol drew several inferences to uphold that case as being correct and made a finding of breach on the back of those inferences[4]. The Defendant sought to appeal these findings, and though the

4 See paragraphs 30 – 43

Supreme Court[5] found them to be "generous" to the Claimant, they declined to interfere with them.

Accordingly, evidential inferences are an integral part of asbestos claims and are an area to be assessed on a case-by-case basis and depending on the evidence which is unearthed and available to the Court.

(iv) Expert Evidence

Another important aspect of breach of duty is expert engineering or hygiene evidence which aims to estimate the extent of a Claimant's exposure. It is customary on any case where breach of duty remains in issue, for such a report to be obtained either on a single joint basis or by each party so as to inform the Court as to the fact, nature and extent of the probable exposure based on the evidence which has been discovered.

Of course, the parameters to which exposure is normally measured, as a first port-of-call, are those as set out in TDN 13 and the subsequent guidance which emerged and which specified 'control limits'. Naturally, this was an important aspect of cases following the decision in *Williams*, discussed above. However, it is now perhaps less important given the legacy of *Bussey*.

Of course, the expert evidence on exposure can only be based on the evidence which has been obtained and which is likely to be before the Court. For those reasons, it is necessary to again repeat and highlight the points made previously about the importance of accurate witness testimony and the utilisation of documentary evidence effectively.

The importance of the role of the engineer is not so much to inform the Court as to whether or not exposure thresholds were repeatedly infringed – as is perhaps more the focus in noise-induced hearing loss claims – but rather, in asbestos claims, it is to inform the Court as to the magnitude of the risk. That is important because, following the line of authority of *Margerson*, *Jeromsom*, and *Bussey*, in particular, that will

5 [2011] UKSC 10 per Lord Phillips at para 166

inform the issue of foreseeability and an assessment of whether the Defendant acted reasonably or not in the circumstances alleged.

To that end, it is of course necessary to consider what measurement ought to be requested from the engineer. This was the source of considerable debate in the case of *Jeromson*:

> *"The judge had first to make findings of fact about that exposure. Before doing so he had to resolve a dispute between counsel as to whether he should be assessing the average or the potential exposure of marine engineers to asbestos dust. He concluded that, given the great variety of experience of individual engineers, a careful employer ought to be addressing his mind to the potential experience of any one of them in deciding what precautions he ought to take."*[6]

The Court of appeal endorsed this aspect of the decision in paragraph 37 of the judgment of Cresswell J:

> *"...where an employer cannot know the extent of any particular employee's exposure over the period of his employment, knows or ought to know that exposure is variable, and knows or ought to know the potential maximum as well as the potential minimum, a reasonable and prudent employer, taking positive thought for the safety of his workers, would have to take thought for the risks involved in the potential maximum exposure. Only if he could be reassured that none of these employees would be sufficiently exposed to be at risk could he safely ignore it."*

Accordingly, it is plain that engineers need to be integrated for maximum exposure levels based on the factual evidence, though it will also be useful for them to provide an average as well. The same will then inform the extent of the likely risk which would have been found on appropriate investigation by the Defendant and then assess what ought to have reasonably have been regarding that risk in the context of the level of knowledge that they will be fixed with at the time the exposure took place.

---

6 Para 36

CHAPTER SIX
TYPES OF ASBESTOS-RELATED INJURY

(i) Introduction

This chapter briefly introduces the types of injuries commonly encountered in asbestos claims, namely; (a) mesothelioma, (b) asbestosis, (c) diffuse pleural thickening, (d) asbestos-induced lung cancer and (e) pleural plaques. All have their special and unique features and legal rules, which are addressed elsewhere in this book in detail.

(ii) Mesothelioma

As Rix LJ introduced the matter in paragraph 1 of Durham v. BAI (Run Off) Limited [2010] EWCA Civ 1096 (Employer's Liability Insurance "Trigger" Litigation):

> *"Mesothelioma is a tragic and fatal disease, so far as is known (but the unknown is never far away in this context) always caused by exposure to asbestos. It manifests itself as a cancer of the mesothelium, a protective lining that covers most of the body's internal organs, but most commonly as a cancer of the pleura, that is to say the linings of the lung. It is unusual in having an extremely long period of gestation, which can be in excess of forty years between exposure to asbestos and manifestation. By the time it has become symptomatic, generally through shortness of breath, the patient does not have long to live, an average of some fourteen months".*

There are a number of striking features to mesothelioma which combine to make it unique.

First, unlike many other occupational diseases, the mechanism by which the disease is caused is not properly understood. As Lord Phillips summarised at paragraph 19 of Sienkiewicz v. Greif (UK) Limited [2011] 2 AC 229:-

> *"i) Mesothelioma is always, or almost always, caused by the inhalation of asbestos fibres.*
>
> *ii) A significant proportion of those who contract mesothelioma have no record of occupational exposure to asbestos. The likelihood is that in their case the disease results from inhalation of asbestos dust that is in the environment. There is, however, a possibility that some cases of mesothelioma are "idiopathic", ie attributable to an unknown cause other than asbestos. Mr Stuart-Smith QC for Greif submitted that the Peto Report indicates that this is more than a possibility, but I do not so read it. I do not, however, think that it matters whether some cases of the disease are idiopathic.*
>
> *iii) The more fibres that are inhaled, the greater the risk of contracting mesothelioma.*
>
> *iv) There is usually a very long period between the exposure to asbestos and the development of the first malignant cell. Typically this can be at least 30 years.*
>
> *v) There will be a lengthy period between the development of the first malignant cell and the point at which the disease can be diagnosed. At the time of Fairchild this was thought to be 10 years, but is now thought to be at least 5 years. During this period, further exposure to asbestos fibres will have no causative effect.*
>
> *vi) The mechanism by which asbestos fibres cause mesothelioma is still not fully understood. It is believed that a cell has to go through 6 or 7 genetic mutations before it becomes malignant, and asbestos fibres may have causative effect on each of these.*
>
> *vii) It is also possible that asbestos fibres have a causative effect by inhibiting the activity of natural killer cells that would otherwise destroy a mutating cell before it reaches the stage of becoming malignant".*

Secondly, associated with this, is the fact that, compared with the other asbestos illnesses, the existence of this particular risk of asbestos exposure was only widely recognised in 1965, only 55 years ago.

Thirdly, there is the peculiarly long time between exposure and the suffering of symptoms, typically being in excess of 30 or 40 years. Compounding that yet further is the fact that for many of those years not only are no symptoms felt, but the disease has not yet wrought the changes upon the body's cells which lead to the subsequent suffering which it causes. As Rix LJ noted at paragraph 3 of *Durham*:-

> *"3. It is important to emphasise that on the current understanding of the disease, it is not present during most of that period of up to four decades. The body's defence mechanisms are extremely efficient in protecting us, and even those who have been most exposed by reason of their occupations, from the potentially harmful effects of the inhalation of asbestos fibres. Only when all those defences have failed may a mutated cell become and remain cancerous and then proceed by exponential growth into the disease called mesothelioma. Even a cancerous mutation may remain dormant for years before it develops into the disease. Or the mutation may actually be reversed by the body's defences, so that the disease never develops. Only a few years ago, the court's view of the expert medical evidence about the onset of mesothelioma was that the disease probably did not occur until approximately ten years before diagnosability (no practical distinction being drawn between diagnosability and manifestation): see Bolton Metropolitan Borough Council v. Municipal Mutual Insurance Ltd [2006] EWCA Civ 50, [2006] 1 WLR 1492 ("Bolton"). In the present case, the judge's view of the more developed expert evidence before him was that that period was closer to only five years before diagnosability. If that is right, then a person exposed to asbestos may live for thirty-five years or thereabouts without passing to a stage at which the court would say that mesothelioma had begun".*

Fourthly, is the fact that even relatively small levels of asbestos exposure can cause mesothelioma, a fact which was widely known since October

1965. As appears from paragraph 54 of the judgment of Jackson LJ in Bussey v. Anglia Heating Limited [2018] EWCA Civ 243:-

> *"From the mid-1960s there was knowledge that exposure to relatively small quantities of asbestos dust, in particular crocidolite, was associated with a risk of developing mesothelioma. It is generally agreed that this became common knowledge in 1965 following publication of an article by Newhouse and Thompson which received national press coverage."*

Fifthly, is the fact that the disease, once it does take hold, is as swift as it is ravaging in its effect, resulting in death usually within shortly over a year from symptoms being experienced, and with it not being unusual for the disease to progress even more rapidly than that. As the case has law has rightly described the illness, in terms of the suffering which it causes, it is both "tragic" and "hideous".

These factors combine to result in a type of litigation which faces peculiar difficulties. The Court is dealing with events which occurred many decades ago, potentially of a very short duration, involving potentially very limited alleged exposures, with a definite procedural urgency, particularly in a living claim. Further, the claims are often of significant value, both in terms of general damages for pain, suffering and loss of amenity and the financial losses associated with a tragic and premature death.

As will be seen from the rest of this book, mesothelioma has resulted in particular principles of breach of duty, causation and procedure.

(iii) Asbestosis

Unlike mesothelioma, asbestosis has been understood to be an injury which asbestos was capable of causing for many years.

As is recorded in paragraph 54 of Jackson LJ's judgment in Bussey:

> *"from the early 1930s there was knowledge that exposure to substantial quantities of asbestos dust was associated with a risk of developing asbestosis".*

As Rix LJ further noted in paragraph 6 of *Durham*:-

> *"The danger of inhaling dust at work has been known about for a considerable time. The classic work on asbestosis in this country lies in the 1930 Report on Effects of Asbestos Dust on the Lungs by Merewether and Price, respectively a medical and engineering inspector of factories. The almost immediate results were the Workmen's Compensation (Silicosis and Asbestosis) Act 1930 and the Asbestos Industry (Asbestosis) Scheme 1931"*

As to the nature of asbestosis, as summarised by the Master of the Rolls in paragraph 2 of Carder v. University of Essex [2016] EWCA Civ 790:

> *"asbestosis is fibrosis of the lung tissue. It is a dose related disease. The asbestos fibres ingested operate cumulatively to cause the disease and then to progress it. The extent and severity of the disease is related to the quantity of fibres ingested. In general, the more fibres ingested, the worse the disease becomes. For that reason, asbestosis is sometimes described as a "divisible" disease".*

Unlike mesothelioma, asbestosis requires much higher levels of asbestos-exposure in order to be caused and safely diagnosed. Commonly "the Helsinki Criteria", first published in 1997, and since updated, are referred to in seeking to determine whether or not exposure has been sufficient for a diagnosis safely to be made. Asbestos is generally associated with relatively high cumulative exposure levels of 25 fibre / ml years together with radiological signs of lung fibrosis.

(iv) Diffuse pleural thickening

Diffuse pleural thickening, like asbestosis, is a dose-related, divisible, condition whereby respiratory disability is caused by thickening of the lining of the lungs caused by asbestos exposure.

As Andrews J recorded in paragraph 21 of McGowan v. Amec Buildings Limited (1 March 2017, High Court), referring to "the Helsinki Criteria":

> *"The 1997 guideline, which was reiterated and confirmed in 2014, says this: "For diffuse pleural thickening, high exposure levels may be required. Bilateral diffuse plate pleural thickening is often associated with moderate or heavy exposure as seen in cases of asbestosis and should be considered accordingly in terms of attribution – i.e. this type of pleural thickening is considered to be close to asbestosis in terms of exposure."*

One of the main differences with pleural thickening is that once symptoms onset – often starting with shortness of breath following relatively low-level exertion – the deterioration is much slower than is the case with asbestos-induced tumours. However, crucially, the sufferer has to live with the risk that such tumours may go onto develop subsequently at any time and that may therefore have a significant effect on their overall life expectancy. Consequently though, pleural thickening claims tend to be 'living claims' at the date of trial with claims for future losses commonly attached for, inter alia; care and assistance, treatment, aids and equipment, and services.

(v) **Asbestos-induced lung cancer**

As is recorded in paragraph 54 of Jackson LJ's judgment in *Bussey*: *"from the mid-1950s there was knowledge of a risk of developing lung cancer"* from asbestos exposure, with one of the experts in that case saying that in 1955 there was identified an increased risk of lung cancer in patients with asbestosis. As will be seen in the chapter on causation, the question of medical causation arising from asbestos exposure is a complicated one, which has attracted special legal principles.

The other factor in relation to asbestos-induced lung cancers, which is different to the other types of asbestos-induced tumours (mesothelioma and asbestos), is that there is often an issue as to whether or not the tumour has another contributing cause. The most common example is where the Claimant has a long-standing smoking history. In such cases therefore, complex issues of causative contribution and apportionment arise since the tumour is often not exclusively caused by asbestos inhalation.

(vi) Pleural plaques

Pleural plaques arise from scar tissue forming in sections of the pleura – the thin membrane of tissues which covers the lungs within the chest cavity. Though there are some changes to the tissue, the effect of pleural plaques is benign and causes no loss or deterioration in lung function. There is, however, a risk of future development of pleural thickening or mesothelioma. This risk does not arise by the plaques themselves turning cancerous – rather it arises from the facts that the plaques are evidence of asbestos inhalation and thus there could be other asbestos fibres within the lungs which could causes cancerous reactions.

In Rothwell v. Chemical and Insulating Co Limited [2009] 1 AC [2008] 1 AC 281, the House of Lords determined that pleural plaques, on their own, could not found a cause of action, because the injury was "de minimis".

Lord Hoffmann explained in paragraph 1 that pleural plaques are:

> *"areas of fibrous thickening of the pleural membrane which surrounds the lungs. Save in very exceptional cases, they cause no symptoms. Nor do they cause other asbestos-related diseases. But they signal the presence in the lungs and pleura of asbestos fibres which may independently cause life-threatening or fatal diseases such as asbestosis or mesothelioma. In consequence, a diagnosis of pleural plaques may cause the patient to contemplate his future with anxiety or even suffer clinical depression".*

Not only can pleural plaques not establish a cause of action on their own, but, as a further result of Rothwell, fear of developing more significant asbestos-related injury, including mesothelioma, and resulting in recognisable psychiatric illness, as a result of developing pleural plaques will not establish a cause of action.

Interestingly, in Scotland[1] and Northern Ireland[2], legislation followed the decision in *Rothwell*, to make pleural plaques actionable injury for which compensation is recoverable. In England and Wales, however, *Rothwell* remains good law. Likewise, despite significant consideration from the Industrial Injuries Advisory Council, pleural plaques remain an injury for which Industrial Injuries Disablement Benefit, is unavailable[3].

1 See Damages (Asbestos-Related Conditions)(Scotland) Act 2009 section 1(2)

2 See Damages (Asbestos-Related Conditions) Act (Northern Ireland) 2011 section 1(1)

3 See IIAC Position Paper 23 published June 2009

CHAPTER SEVEN
CAUSATION IN ASBESTOS CLAIMS

(i) Introduction

Causation has proven to be a particularly complicated concept in asbestos claims, not least because there are different causation rules for each different type of injury. This chapter will address the different rules which apply for (a) mesothelioma claims, (b) asbestosis and diffuse pleural thickening claims, and (c) asbestos-induced lung cancer claims.

We will now look at how the legal principles of causation have been developed and applied by the Courts in relation to each type of asbestos-related injury.

(ii) Mesothelioma

Mesothelioma confronted the law with the stark question of how to deal with causation of a disease in relation to which the precise mechanism of medical causation is not understood. In particular, if there were multiple sources of exposure, it was scientifically impossible to say which had actually medically caused the mesothelioma.

In Sienkiewicz v. Greif (UK) Limited [2011] 2 AC 229 Lord Phillips explained conventional causation principles in disease claims as follows:-

> *"16. It is a basic principle of the law of tort that the claimant will only have a cause of action if he can prove, on balance of probabilities, that the defendant's tortious conduct caused the damage in respect of which compensation is claimed. He must show that, but for the defendant's tortious conduct he would not have suffered the damage. This broad test of balance of probabilities means that in some cases a defendant will be held liable for damage which he did*

not, in fact, cause. Equally there will be cases where the defendant escapes liability, notwithstanding that he has caused the damage, because the claimant is unable to discharge the burden of proving causation. There is an important exception to the "but for" test. Where disease is caused by the cumulative effect of the inhalation of dust, part of which is attributable to breach of duty on the part of the defendant and part of which involves no breach of duty, the defendant will be liable on the ground that his breach of duty has made a material contribution to the disease – Bonnington Castings Ltd v Wardlaw [1956] AC 613 ...".

The legal difficulty with mesothelioma, is, as explained by Lord Phillips in paragraph 19 of *Sienkiewicz*, that, although much is understood about mesothelioma, the mechanism by which the disease is caused is still not fully understood:-

"i) Mesothelioma is always, or almost always, caused by the inhalation of asbestos fibres.

ii) A significant proportion of those who contract mesothelioma have no record of occupational exposure to asbestos. The likelihood is that in their case the disease results from inhalation of asbestos dust that is in the environment. There is, however, a possibility that some cases of mesothelioma are "idiopathic", ie attributable to an unknown cause other than asbestos. Mr Stuart-Smith QC for Greif submitted that the Peto Report indicates that this is more than a possibility, but I do not so read it. I do not, however, think that it matters whether some cases of the disease are idiopathic.

iii) The more fibres that are inhaled, the greater the risk of contracting mesothelioma.

iv) There is usually a very long period between the exposure to asbestos and the development of the first malignant cell. Typically this can be at least 30 years.

v) There will be a lengthy period between the development of the first malignant cell and the point at which the disease can be diagnosed.

At the time of Fairchild this was thought to be 10 years, but is now thought to be at least 5 years. During this period, further exposure to asbestos fibres will have no causative effect.

vi) The mechanism by which asbestos fibres cause mesothelioma is still not fully understood. It is believed that a cell has to go through 6 or 7 genetic mutations before it becomes malignant, and asbestos fibres may have causative effect on each of these.

vii) It is also possible that asbestos fibres have a causative effect by inhibiting the activity of natural killer cells that would otherwise destroy a mutating cell before it reaches the stage of becoming malignant".

This lack of understanding of the mechanism by which asbestos fibres cause mesothelioma, however, meant that, on conventional "but for" causation principles a Claimant who had been exposed to multiple sources of asbestos would be unable to prove that any particular party who had exposed him or her to asbestos was responsible for his or her illness. On conventional principles, therefore, even if a party who had, in breach of duty, exposed the Claimant to substantial and reasonably foreseeably hazardous (even by reference to the standards of the time of exposure) levels of asbestos, the claim against that party would fail on causation. Given the nature of the injury and its catastrophic effect on Claimants, plainly an unjust situation presented itself. Likewise for the Defendant whose wrongful exposure, in actual fact, had not caused the mesothelioma, there was the risk that they would foot the bill for the negligent Defendant whose exposure had done.

That caused the Courts to consider an exception for mesothelioma cases. In Fairchild v Glenhaven Funeral Services Ltd [2003] 1 AC 32, the House of Lords determined that when a victim contracts mesothelioma each person who has, in breach of duty, been responsible for exposing the victim to a significant quantity of asbestos dust and thus creating a "material increase in risk" of the victim contracting the disease will be held to be jointly and severally liable for causing the disease.

Lord Bingham drew upon the analogy of the "two hunters problem":-

> *"Take the well-known example where two hunters, acting independently of each other, fire their guns carelessly in a wood, and a pellet from one of the guns injures an innocent passer-by. No one knows, and the plaintiff is unable to prove, from which gun the pellet came. Should the law of negligence leave the plaintiff remediless, and allow both hunters to go away scot-free, even though one of them must have fired the injurious pellet? Not surprisingly, the courts have declined to reach such an unjust decision … As between the plaintiff and the two hunters, the evidential difficulty arising from the impossibility of identifying the gun which fired the crucial pellet should redound upon the negligent hunters, not the blameless plaintiff. The unattractive consequence, that one of the hunters will be held liable for an injury he did not in fact inflict, is outweighed by the even less attractive alternative, that the innocent plaintiff should receive no recompense even though one of the negligent hunters injured him. It is this balance ('..outweighed by..') which justifies a relaxation in the standard of causation required. Insistence on the normal standard of causation would work an injustice. Hunting in a careless manner and thereby creating a risk of injury to others, followed by injury to another person, is regarded by the law as sufficient causal connection in the circumstances to found responsibility".*

As was recognised explicitly by Lord Bingham in Fairchild, *"this balancing exercise involves a value judgment"*. The Court's value judgment was that the greater injustice would be for the negligently exposed Claimant to recover nothing, when compared to the negligently exposing Defendant in relation to whom it could not medically said that the fibres for which that employer was responsible caused the mesothelioma.

The *Fairchild* principle was further refined and developed in Barker v Corus UK Ltd [2006] 2 AC 572. The House of Lords held that each employer was liable only for that proportion of the damages which represented its contribution to the total risk that the employee would contract mesothelioma. Practically, the Court considered that it was unfair to hold an employer liable for the whole of the injury in cases where there is only a small chance (due to a small exposure, compared to other exposures) that the employer caused the injury. Theoretically, the limiting of the principle was justified by interpreting the *Fairchild* principle as one that rendered a defendant liable for contributing to risk, not contributing to injury. The risk created was itself the damage, albeit that the principle only applied where injury had been caused. As risk or chance was infinitely divisible, each defendant could be held liable for his contribution to the risk.

For the purposes of causation, as Lord Hoffmann explained:

> *"it should be irrelevant whether the other exposure was tortious or non-tortious, by natural causes or human agency or by the claimant himself. These distinctions may be relevant to whether and to whom responsibility can also be attributed, but from the point of view of satisfying the requirement of a sufficient causal link between the defendant's conduct and the claimant's injury, they should not matter."*

As to how the injury would be apportioned between responsible causes, Lord Hoffmann said the following at paragraph 48:-

> *"But when the damage is apportioned among the persons responsible for the exposures to asbestos which created the risk, it is known that those exposures were together sufficient to cause the disease. The damages which would have been awarded against a defendant who had actually caused the disease must be apportioned to the defendants according to their contributions to the risk. It may be that the most practical method of apportionment will be according to the time of exposure for which each defendant is responsible, but allowance may have to be made for the intensity of exposure and the type of asbestos. These questions are not before the House and it is to be hoped that the parties, their insurers and advisers will devise practical and economical criteria for dealing with them.".*

Parliament reacted swiftly to *Barker* and enacted Section 3 of the Compensation Act 2006, which had retrospective effect, applying to all cases which had not been determined or settled prior to the date of the decision in Barker (3 May 2006). Section 3 made all tortfeasors who had materially increased the risk of mesothelioma jointly and severally liable for the whole of the injury:-

(1) This section applies where—

(a) a person ('the responsible person') has negligently or in breach of statutory duty caused or permitted another person ('the victim') to be exposed to asbestos,

(b) the victim has contracted mesothelioma as a result of exposure to asbestos,

(c) because of the nature of mesothelioma and the state of medical science, it is not possible to determine with certainty whether it was the exposure mentioned in paragraph (a) or another exposure which caused the victim to become ill, and

(d) the responsible person is liable in tort, by virtue of the exposure mentioned in paragraph (a), in connection with damage caused to the victim by the disease (whether by reason of having materially increased a risk or for any other reason).

(2) The responsible person shall be liable—

(a) in respect of the whole of the damage caused to the victim by the disease (irrespective of whether the victim was also exposed to asbestos —

> *(i) other than by the responsible person, whether or not in circumstances in which another person has liability in tort, or*
>
> *(ii) by the responsible person in circumstances in which he has no liability in tort), and*

(b) jointly and severally with any other responsible person."

Section 3, however, did expressly leave open apportionment between tortfeasors. So, a tortfeasor liable for the whole of the injury to the Claimant could recover a contribution from other tortfeasors. It placed, however, the risk of tracing and pursuing such other tortfeasors upon the Defendant, together with the risk of such party being insolvent or lacking traceable insurance. In this regard, by Sub-section 3(4), the default method of apportionment between Defendants was stated to be the relative periods of duration of exposure, but it was open to the parties to agree, or the Court to find, another appropriate way of apportionment:-

"(4) In determining the extent of contributions of different responsible persons in accordance with subsection (3)(a), a court shall have regard to the relative lengths of the periods of exposure for which each was responsible; but this subsection shall not apply—

"if or to the extent that responsible persons agree to apportion responsibility amongst themselves on some other basis, or

if or to the extent that the court thinks that another basis for determining contributions is more appropriate in the circumstances of a particular case".

Further, Section 3 left open arguments of contributory negligence, such that the Claimant's damages could potentially be reduced if his or own (negligent) self-exposure (such as in self-employment, or working on DIY / home projects) constituted some of his or her own exposure.

In *Sienkiewicz*, the Court addressed what was a "material increase in the risk" at paragraphs 107 – 108, per Lord Phillips:-

"107. Liability for mesothelioma falls on anyone who has materially increased the risk of the victim contracting the disease. What constitutes a material increase of risk? The parties were, I think, agreed that the insertion of the word "material" is intended to exclude an increase of risk that is so insignificant that the court will properly disregard it on the de minimis principle. ...

108. I doubt whether it is ever possible to define, in quantitative terms, what for the purposes of the application of any principle of law, is de minimis. This must be a question for the judge on the facts of the particular case. In the case of mesothelioma, a stage must be reached at which, even allowing for the possibility that exposure to asbestos can have a cumulative effect, a particular exposure is too insignificant to be taken into account, having regard to the overall exposure that has taken place. The question is whether that is the position in this case".

(iii) Asbestosis and asbestos-induced diffuse pleural thickening

Asbestosis and pleural thickening proved less complex in conceptual terms, applying purely conventional historical principles. These injuries were "divisible", "dose-related" conditions, where each exposure contributed to the overall injury by reference to the extent of the exposure in question compared to total, lifetime, exposure. The law has accepted that it is sufficient for the Claimant to prove a material contribution to a more than "de minimis" overall injury.

As Lord Phillips explained in paragraph 14 of *Sienkiewicz*, asbestosis is a divisible and dose-related condition:-

"The agent ingested operates cumulatively first to cause the disease and then to progress the disease. Thus the severity of the disease is related to the quantity of the agent that is ingested … For this reason it is important to distinguish between asbestosis and mesothelioma when considering principles of causation"

Anthony Edis QC, sitting as a Deputy Judge of the High Court, in Dowdall v. William Kenyon & Sons Limited [2014] EHWC 2822 (QB), said further at paragraph 12:-

"Asbestosis is a divisible injury in the sense that the injury varies in severity depending on the extent of exposure. In Holtby v Brigham & Cowan (Hull) Limited [2000] ICR 1086, the Court of Appeal held that in an asbestosis case a defendant was only liable for that part of

the injury attributable to the tortious exposure for which that defendant was responsible. Further, that the burden of proving what part of the injury was caused by a particular defendant lay on the claimant. In these circumstances, it is incumbent on a claimant to trace all the previous employers responsible for his asbestos exposure and, given that many such employers are no longer viable companies, to trace their insurers during each relevant period of employment".

Expert written medical evidence will have to be led to prove the diagnosis and causation of asbestosis as a condition, and to distinguish it from other non-asbestos related causes of pulmonary fibrosis or thickening, and, in particular, idiopathic pulmonary fibrosis. Medical experts often accept that "the Helsinki Criteria" (first produced in 1997) have to be established in the case of asbestosis, including importantly that the Claimant's overall lifetime exposure to asbestos was greater than 25 fibre / ml years. This has been discussed in the previous Chapter.

Medical causation of diffuse pleural thickening has similarly to be addressed on its own expert written medical evidence. As Andrews J found in McGowan v. Amec Buildings Limited (1 March 2017, High Court), it is likely to be necessary to show exposure to sufficiently high lifetime levels of asbestos safely to prove medical causation.

Subject to proof of medical causation, however, a Defendant is liable for the proportion of the total exposure attributable to the tortious exposure for which that defendant was responsible. The burden of proof is upon the Claimant. It is for the Defendant to raise the issue of apportionment, but the outcome rarely depends upon burden of proof, but rather upon deciding the contribution made by various sources on the evidence. Generally, a time-exposed basis (just as with mesothelioma apportionment) is the correct way to proceed. Stuart-Smith LJ, at paragraph 20 of Holtby v. Brigham and Cowan (Hull) Limited [2000] ICR 1086, said that:-

"the onus of proving causation is on the claimant; it does not shift to the defendant. He will be entitled to succeed if he can prove that the defendant's tortious conduct made a material contribution to his dis-

> *ability. But strictly speaking the defendant is liable only to the extent of that contribution. However, if the point is never raised or argued by the defendant, the claimant will succeed in full as in Bonnington Castings Ltd v Wardlaw [1956] A.C. 613 and McGhee v National Coal Board [1973] 1 WLR 1. I agree with Judge Altman that strictly speaking the defendant does not need to plead that others were responsible in part. But at the same time I certainly think it is desirable and preferable that this should be done. Certainly the matter must be raised and dealt with in evidence, otherwise the defendant is at risk that he will be held liable for everything. In reality I do not think that these cases should be determined on onus of proof. The question should be whether at the end of the day, and on consideration of all the evidence, the claimant has proved that the defendant is responsible for the whole or a quantifiable part of his disability. The question of quantification may be difficult and the court only has to do the best it can using its common sense ... Cases of this sort, where the disease manifests itself many years after the exposure, present great problems, because much of the detail is inevitably lost. ... But, in my view, the court must do the best it can to achieve justice, not only to the claimant but also to the defendant, and among defendants."*
>
> *23. Further, at paragraph 25, Stuart-Smith LJ confirmed the position re the time-exposed basis of apportionment as follows:- "This method of dividing responsibility on a time exposure basis is, I understand, adopted among insurers in such cases as these. In the absence of some unusual feature, such as for example periods of exposure to a particularly dangerous blue asbestos during some periods, that seems to me to be not only the sensible, but the correct approach in law. In practice, many years afterwards, such distinctions are likely to be impossible to prove."*

The divisible nature of the injury and approach to apportionment has, however, led to particular arguments about whether or not small periods of employment, leading to a small contribution to overall exposure, are "de minimis". This was first addressed by His Honour Judge Gore QC, sitting as a Judge of the High Court, in Carder v. University of Essex [2015] EWHC 2399 (QB), who held that a 2.3% contribution to an injury which was overall more than "de minimis" was itself not "de minimis". Cox J reached the same conclusion in Mayne v. Atlas Stone Company Limited [2016] EWHC 1030 (QB). The Court of Appeal considered the *Carder* case in [2016] EWCA Civ 790. At paragraph 26, the Court said that the principle was as follows:-

> *"To summarise, the question whether a claimant has suffered material (i.e. more than negligible) damage in an asbestosis case where he has been exposed to more than one source of asbestos dust raises no difficulties of principle. It depends on the facts of the particular case. In the court below, it was said that the appellant's point (viz that the breach of duty caused no actionable injury in this case) was "novel" in an asbestosis case. I do not consider that this case raises a novel point of law or principle. That is not to say that resolving the question of fact on the evidence in this case is straightforward".*

The Court of Appeal upheld on the facts the decision reached at first instance.

Accordingly, therefore, in claims for asbestosis or diffuse pleural thickening, the material contribution to risk test as per *Fairchild*, remains the relevant test for causation. However, unlike with mesothelioma, there is no Compensation Act equivalent provision enabling a Claimant to recover in full from just one Defendant. Rather, the Claimant can only recover a proportion of his claim from each Defendant against whom he proves causative breach, and the remainder of his damages will go unrecovered unless another Defendant can be successfully pursued.

(iv) Asbestos-induced lung cancer

Asbestos-induced lung cancer has resulted in a neat theoretical "halfway house", applying the causation rules appropriate to a mesothelioma claim, but without the statutory intervention of the Compensation Act 2006, showing what asbestos litigation in mesothelioma claims would have been like if Parliament had not intervened in the field of causation.

The medical evidence in a case will have to establish whether or not, medically, lung cancer can be attributed to asbestos exposure. As with asbestos, this is often approached by reference to "the Helsinki Criteria (as occurred in the case of Heneghan v. Manchester Dry Docks Limited [2016] 1 WLR 2036 – referred to below).

The Court of Appeal in *Heneghan* applied at paragraphs 46 and 47, the *Fairchild* approach to asbestos-induced lung cancer. If the lung cancer could be attributed to asbestos, it was sufficient to prove a case against an individual Defendant that the Defendant materially increased the risk of developing lung cancer. It was not necessary for the Claimant to prove that a particular exposure probably caused the lung cancer:-

> *"That test is to be applied where the court is satisfied on scientific evidence that the exposure for which the defendant is responsible has in fact contributed to the injury. This is readily demonstrated in the case of divisible injuries (such as silicosis and pneumoconiosis) whose severity is proportionate to the amount of exposure to the causative agent. 47. The response of the law to the problem posed in a case where the scientific evidence does not permit a finding that the exposure attributable to a particular defendant contributed to the injury is to apply the Fairchild exception. The factors identified in Fairchild for the application of this solution exist in the present case: (i) all the defendants concede their breach of duty; (ii) all increased the risk that the deceased would contract lung cancer; (iii) all exposed the deceased to the same agency that was implicated in causation (asbestos fibres); but (iv) medical science is unable to determine to which (if any) of the defendants there should be attributed the exposure which actually caused the cell changes which initiated the genetic changes culminating in the cancer".*

Just as the *Fairchild* approach applied, however, so did the refinement of *Barker*: damages were to be apportioned by reference to the proportionate contribution made by the Defendant's tortious exposure as compared to the total global exposure. Again, there is no Compensation Act 2006 equivalent provision which applies to asbestos-related lung cancer claims. As such, as per *Barker* and *Holtby*, recovering full compensation can only be achieved when all Defendants are successfully pursued, and each Defendant will only pay out for the extent of their contribution to the increase in risk.

The other peculiarity to asbestos-related lung cancer cases is apportionment with other non-asbestos contributors to the injury. In short, medical science is unable to determine the extent to which a lung cancer tumour is caused by asbestos, or other non-asbestos agents such as smoking or idiopathic ailments. All that the science can say is that exposure to asbestos doubles the risk of such a tumour developing. On that basis, a Court will likely be satisfied that any material exposure to asbestos has contributed to the development of the injury, but, equally, it may the case that it has not caused the full extent of the injury. It is therefore often the case that Defendants will seek to discount damages for those other potential contributions to the development of the tumour. The most common is where the Claimant has a smoking history of some significance and the Defendant alleges that the Claimant is guilty of contributory negligence.

The Court has set itself against simply apportioning mathematically in cases of contributory negligence by the proportions by which exposure to asbestos and smoking increased the risk of contracting lung cancer. In Department for Communities and Local Government v. Blackmore [2017] EWCA Civ 1136 the Court of Appeal said[1] that "*the correct approach to the assessment of contributory negligence was, to my mind, helpfully summarised by Stanley Burnton J., as he then was, in Badger v. Ministry of Defence [2005] EWHC 2941 as follows (at [16]): "… [O]nce contributory negligence has been established, the court must take into account both the extent of the claimant's responsibility for his injury and damage and the blameworthiness of his conduct as opposed to that of the defendant in deciding on the reduction in damages that is just and equitable. The decision as to the appropriate reduction in the claimant's damages is to be dealt with in a broad, jury like and common sense way: …*"

1 Paragraph 38

This involves consideration of not just the causative impact of smoking and asbestos exposure, but also the parties' respective blameworthiness. As the Court continued[2], "*there is a particular policy underlying Parliament's strict prohibition of the exposure of workers to asbestos and other harmful substances which needs to be reflected in the apportionment of responsibility*". Accordingly, "*the judge was right to give very considerable weight to the blameworthiness of the employer in exposing its employee to asbestos in breach of a strict statutory duty in circumstances where the dangers of asbestos to health were well known. By comparison, a lesser degree of blame attaches to the conduct of Mr. Blackmore in continuing to smoke after the dangers of smoking to health became known*".

2 Paragraph 39

CHAPTER EIGHT
DAMAGES

This Chapter will be split into three parts to try and focus the prevalent issues relevant to asbestos claims. The first part will focus on the levels and calculations of awards which are normally engaged in cases of asbestos-related injury. The second part will focus on the particular issues which arise in those cases where the Claimant has sadly passed away from the injury which is the subject of the claim. To that end, we will look briefly at damages under the Fatal Accidents Act 1976 and Law Reform (Miscellaneous Provisions) Act 1934 and the relevant elements of special and consequential damage which often form part of these claims. Finally, we will consider those 'living' claims where the Claimant is still alive and will need long-term care or treatment as a result of their injury and how such claims are normally structured and dealt with by the Courts.

PART ONE – DAMAGES FOR PAIN, SUFFERING AND LOSS OF AMENITY

(i) Introduction

The starting point in any case is the Judicial College Guidelines for the Assessment of General Damages in Personal Injury Cases (currently in its 15th Edition, 2019), Section 6(C), which specifically addresses asbestos-related disease, which separate sub-divisions for the different types of disease.

Any proper assessment of damages will require careful attention to, and analysis of, the evidence in the case, and in particular the expert medical evidence. The main issues are addressed below.

(ii) Uplifts on damages for PSLA

Following Simmons v. Castle [2013] EWCA Civ 1039 general damages for pain, suffering and loss of amenity have, with effect from 1 April 2013, been 10% higher than that they previously would have been, unless a conditional fee agreement which permits recovery of a success fee against the Defendant has been entered into.

Due to Section 44 of the Legal Aid, Sentencing and Punishment of Offenders Act 2012, in all personal injury claims other than "*proceedings relating to a claim for damages in respect of diffuse mesothelioma*", where a conditional fee agreement which provides for a success fee was entered into after 1 April 2013, that success fee is not recoverable against the Defendant and the 10% *Simmons v. Castle* uplift applies.

Mesothelioma, however, is a special case, because the Conditional Fee Agreements Order 2013 has transitional provisions which mean that in mesothelioma claims, a success fee can still be recovered in respect of a conditional fee agreement which has been entered into even after 1 April 2013. If such a conditional fee agreement is entered into, however, the 10% *Simmons v. Castle* uplift does not apply.

(iii) Mesothelioma claims

As noted above, if there is a conditional fee agreement which provides for recovery of a success fee, the 10% *Simmons v. Castle* uplift will not apply.

Mesothelioma claims, as a category of cases, attract the highest awards of all of the categories of asbestos claims.

Regard must be had to whatever edition of the Judicial College Guidelines for the Assessment of General Damages in Personal Injury Cases which is in force at the date of assessment of damages, because the guidelines are periodically updated. However, as at the date of publication the range of awards (without the 10% uplift, because generally there will be a conditional fee agreement in force which provides for a success fee) is £59,730 – £107,410[1].

The factors particularly specified, as to where in the range the award, should fall, include the following:-

(1) The duration of pain and suffering. Often the disease is fatal within months of diagnosis and within around a year of first symptoms being experienced. It is not unusual for the duration of the illness to be shorter, or a little longer.

(2) The nature and extent of the investigations undertaken (for example, has there been a surgical procedure such as thoracoscopy – "*keyhole*" surgical insertion of an exploratory camera).

(3) The nature and extent of treatment, including surgical treatment (such as pleurectomy / decortication – the surgical removal of the lung lining and tumour masses – or talc pleurodesis – the insertion of "*talc*" to prevent fluid building up in the lining of the lung), chemotherapy and radiotherapy (with it being not unusual to encounter cases where these are attempted, or not attempted at all, depending upon the judgment made by

1 As per the 15th Edition of the Guidelines

patients and clinicians as to the likely benefits and impact on quality of life).

(4) The spread of the tumour, both; (a) to encase the lungs or (b) to involve other organs (with it not being unusual for the tumour to metastasise and spread to other organs).

(5) The impact on life expectancy. This is usually addressed by the expert written medical evidence, which should include; (a) the prognosis and life expectancy with the disease and (b) the life expectancy but for developing mesothelioma (which is usually addressed by taking a statistical average for age and gender and then reducing or increasing the same having regard to comorbid medical state of health – state of health prior to and disregarding mesothelioma – and important habits such as smoking). This can be an important factor due to the significant age range of persons suffering from mesothelioma, with the usual range, due to the long period of latency of the disease, being from people in their 50s all the way up to people in their late 80s.

(6) Impact on enjoyment of family life and enjoyment of life. The importance of this factor will depend upon the particular facts of a case but the authors of this book venture to suggest that, sadly, the circumstances will always be tragic, involving as it always does the curtailing and shortening of life, which will always have a significant effect on others.

(iv) Asbestos-induced lung cancer

Again, regard must be had to whatever edition of the Judicial College Guidelines for the Assessment of General Damages in Personal Injury Cases which is in force at the date of assessment of damages, because the guidelines are periodically updated. However, as at the date of publication the range of awards (with the 10% uplift, because, unless there is a conditional fee agreement which provides for a success fee which was entered into before 1 April 2013 – which will be a rarity, and probably only in an old provisional damages case, the 10% *Simmons v. Castle* uplift applies) is £59,730 – £83,050.

The same kind of factor as with mesothelioma are relevant to determining where in the range the award should fall. The Guidelines specifically note that, although the symptoms of lung cancer may be less painful, but more protracted, than mesothelioma, there are cases of lung cancer which result in a similar level of suffering to mesothelioma, such as to justify an award above the range.

(v) Asbestosis and diffuse pleural thickening

Depending upon comorbid state of medical health, a person may live for many years with asbestosis or diffuse pleural thickening, once symptoms manifest. The disease may or may not be the cause of death of a sufferer. There is a wide range of levels of disability associated with the disease and prognoses (which depends generally upon the rate of progression, which is, as a matter of generality, usually relatively slow in the case of asbestosis).

This leads to a very large range of awards, on the current edition of the Judicial College Guidelines for the Assessment of General Damages in Personal Injury Cases, spanning from £14,140 (with the 10% uplift, for the same reasons as set out above in relation to asbestos-induced lung cancer) to £99,330, with the Guidelines specifically noting that there are cases of asbestosis which result in a similar level of suffering to mesothelioma, such as to justify an award above the range.

The main factors in determining the levels of award are:-

(1) The level of respiratory disability attributable to the disease (measured usually in percentage terms).

(2) The prognosis for the progression of the disease, in terms of future disability.

(3) The impact (of (1) and (2) upon quality of life).

(4) Whether or not the award is made on a provisional damages basis (with typical return conditions including mesothelioma and asbestos-induced lung cancer, and with more controversial return conditions including further progression of asbestos / diffuse pleural thickening – with it often being hard to specify an appropriately clear, measurable and specific, and appropriately serious, deterioration in condition to represent a viable return condition).

(vi) Evidence relevant to the assessment of PSLA

The following are crucial sources of evidence which the Court will have regard to in assessment PSLA damages in asbestos-related injury claims:

- Witness evidence – the Claimant's evidence, and the evidence of family and friends, as to how their condition has deteriorated, and the impact that has had on their ability to perform their normal day-to-day activities is very important. Likewise, descriptions of treatment and investigative procedures and pain and discomfort is also important.
- The Claimant's medical records ought also to be obtained. They will likely demonstrate the investigations since onset which have occurred and it will be possible to build a picture as to the speed of deterioration and contemporaneous impact of the injury on the Claimant's health generally.
- Expert medical evidence. Plainly, this will be the primary source for any aspect and it should draw on the other types of evidence listed above. It is imperative that the expert makes comparisons of the Claimant's health before and after the onset of symptoms and how the injury has impacted upon life expectancy and the Claimant's quality of life at the time of assessment and going forward.

PART TWO – ISSUES IN FATAL CLAIMS

(i) Introduction

A fatal claim, brought after the death of the sufferer, will almost always encompass a claim on behalf of the estate of the Deceased, under Section 1 of the Law Reform (Miscellaneous Provisions) Act 1934. It will also, in a case in which the Deceased had (a) a spouse or civil partner (who was living at the time of death and is still alive at the time of assessment of damages) and / or (b) a dependant or dependants (as defined in Section 1 of the Fatal Accidents Act 1976) (whether or not that dependant, or those dependants, is or include a spouse or civil partner of the Deceased), who were dependent upon the Deceased financially or in respect of services, be usual for there to be a claim under the Fatal Accidents Act 1976. This section addresses the issues to be addressed in damages claims in both of those aspects of a fatal claim.

(ii) Claims on behalf of the estate of the Deceased under the 1934 Act

(a) Survival of the Deceased's cause of action

Under Section 1 of the 1934 Act, "*all causes of action subsisting against or vested in* [a Deceased person] *shall survive against, or, as the case may be, for the benefit of, his estate*".

Importantly, the disease in respect of which the claim is brought does not need to be the cause of death, although in a mesothelioma claim it is almost always the cause of death. Even in a case in which the Deceased died for entirely unrelated reasons (such as in a road traffic accident), the cause of action survives for the benefit of the estate.

(b) Standing to sue: executors and administrators

The claim must be brought by the Deceased's executors (if he or she had a will) or administrators (if he or she died intestate).

If there is a will, the executors can sue without first obtaining a grant of probate, but will need to obtain and produce the grant of probate before judgment is obtained:- per Rimer LJ in Millburn-Snell v. Evans [2012] 1 WLR 41 "*whereas an executor derives his title to sue from the will and not from the grant of probate and so can validly sue before obtaining a grant (although he will have to obtain it later in order to prove his title)*"[2].

The position in the case of a person who dies intestate is, in this respect, entirely different, however. A claim purportedly issued on behalf of the estate of a Deceased person before letters of administration have been granted is a nullity which cannot be cured even by the subsequent grant of letters of administration. Please see Rimer LJ again in *Millburn-Snell.* A claim issued purportedly by administrators of an intestate estate prior to the granting of letters of administration "*was a nullity that must be struck out and could not be retrospectively validated by a grant of letters of administration. ... an administrator derives his title to sue solely from the grant of administration*".

(c) **Heads of loss recoverable**

The heads of loss which are recoverable, and typically claimed are:-

(1) General damages for pain, suffering and loss of amenity.

(2) Funeral expenses.

(3) Financial losses suffered between the date of onset of the illness and the date of death.

General damages for pain, suffering and loss of amenity

There are no special principles applicable to the assessment of general damages for pain, suffering and loss of amenity in personal injury cases in fatal cases. The general principles apply. Those general principles are

2 Paragraph 14

addressed in the preceding part. In a fatal case the facts are fully known and there is no uncertainty over prognosis and progression of the disease. Assessment of general damages in such cases is fundamentally a question of assessing the course and impact of the disease, including upon life expectancy.

Funeral expenses

Such expenses are only recoverable if the tort caused the Deceased's death.

As noted in Grant v. Secretary of State for Transport [2017] EWHC 1663 (QB)[3]:-

(1) Expenses in the nature of a wake or reception are, in principle, irrecoverable.

(2) The cost of a headstone is, in principle recoverable.

(3) The sums which are in principle recoverable are only recoverable to the extent that is reasonable.

It is not unusual for claims to be made for items such as flowers and advertisements.

What is a reasonable may well be a difficult issue to decide if there is a serious dispute over the same.

(iii) Claims under the Fatal Accidents Act 1976

(a) Preconditions for a claim

Under Section 1(1) of the 1976 Act, it is necessary for the Claimant(s) to prove that (a) the Deceased's death was caused by the tort and (b) that the there was a tort which the Deceased could have sued for had he or she not died. (a) is a significant and important departure from the

3 Paragraphs 53 – 55, per Mr. Martin Chamberlain QC, as he then was

position under the 1934 Act, under which it is not necessary for the Deceased to have died by reason of the tort for the estate to maintain a claim in respect of the pre-death consequences of the tort:-

> *"(1) If death is caused by any wrongful act, neglect or default which is such as would (if death had not ensued) have entitled the person injured to maintain an action and recover damages in respect thereof, the person who would have been liable if death had not ensued shall be liable to an action for damages, notwithstanding the death of the person injured".*

Under Section 2 of the 1976 Act, the action shall be brought by and in the name of the executor or administrator of the deceased. Further, not more than one action shall lie for and in respect of the same subject matter of complaint.

As to the persons on whose behalf the claim may be brought by the executors or administrators of the Deceased's estate, Section 1(2) of the 1976 Act provides that "*every such action shall be for the benefit of the dependants of the person ("the deceased") whose death has been so caused*"

The list of "*dependants*" is to be found in Section 1(3) of the 1976 Act:-

> *"(3) In this Act " dependant " means—*
>
> *(a) the wife or husband or former wife or husband of the deceased;*
>
> *(aa) the civil partner or former civil partner of the deceased;*
>
> *(b) any person who—*
>
> > *(i) was living with the deceased in the same household immediately before the date of the death; and*
> >
> > *(ii) had been living with the deceased in the same household for at least two years before that date; and*
> >
> > *(iii) was living during the whole of that period as the husband or wife or civil partner of the deceased;*

(c) any parent or other ascendant of the deceased;

(d) any person who was treated by the deceased as his parent;

(e) any child or other descendant of the deceased;

(f) any person (not being a child of the deceased) who, in the case of any marriage to which the deceased was at any time a party, was treated by the deceased as a child of the family in relation to that marriage;

(fa) any person (not being a child of the deceased) who, in the case of any civil partnership in which the deceased was at any time a civil partner, was treated by the deceased as a child of the family in relation to that civil partnership;

(g) any person who is, or is the issue of, a brother, sister, uncle or aunt of the deceased".

(b) **Special cause of action: bereavement**

Under Section 1A of the 1976 Act a husband, wife or civil partner whose marriage or civil partnership to the Deceased is subsisting at the time of death is entitled to a bereavement award of £15,120 if the death occurred on or after 1 May 2020 and £12,980 if the death occurred prior to that date.

An important point which may be thought by the reader to be anachronistic is that, despite the Court of Appeal declaring in Smith v. Lancashire Teaching Hospitals NHS Foundation Trust [2018] QB 804 that it was incompatible with the European Convention on Human Rights and the Human Rights Act 1998 that bereavement award is available only to persons who are married or in a civil partnership, and not available to persons who, whilst formally unmarried, had been cohabiting in the same household as husband or wife, for at least 2 years (and were accordingly otherwise "*dependents*" under Section 1(3), as addressed above), Parliament has still not amended Section 1A to provide for a claim for such persons and to put them in the same position as persons in a marriage or civil partnership.

Another important point to note is that, pursuant to Section 1(1A) of the 1934 Act, "*the right of a person to claim under section 1A of the Fatal Accidents Act 1976 (bereavement) shall not survive for the benefit of his estate on his death*". This means that if the surviving spouse or civil partner dies before damages are assessed, the claim for the bereavement award lapses with their death and does not survive for the benefit of their estate.

(c) **Other heads of claim under the 1976 Act**

Under Section 3(1) of the 1976 Act "*in the action such damages, other than damages for bereavement, may be awarded as are proportioned to the injury resulting from the death to the dependants respectively*".

Funeral expenses

If and insofar as the funeral expenses are not claimed and recovered in the 1934 Act claim by the estate, funeral expenses can be recovered by reason of Section 3(5) of the 1976 Act:- "*if the dependants have incurred funeral expenses in respect of the deceased, damages may be awarded in respect of those expenses*". The principles are addressed above in respect of a 1934 Act claim.

Loss of financial dependency

The task is to assess what, if any, dependency the dependant had upon the Deceased financially and; (a) for what period of time the Deceased would, but for the tort, have been able and willing to provide for the dependency and (b) for what period of time the dependent would, but for the tort, have been able to receive the benefit. The period of recovery is limited to the shorter of those 2 periods.

Accordingly, it is necessary to consider, in an alleged long-term dependency, typically found between spouses, civil partners and long-term cohabiting domestic partners, the life expectancy of the Deceased and what sources of income he or she would have had, together with how long the dependant would have been able to receive the benefit. Accordingly, for example, if the life expectancy of the dependent, at the time of death of the Deceased, is 10 years, and the Deceased would, but for the tort, only have been able to provide for the dependency (by reason of his or her own life expectancy) for another 5 years, the period of loss is 5 years.

The conventional principle, in the case of persons who are married / in a civil partnership / cohabiting, who pool their finances, following Harris v. Empress Motors Limited [1984] 1 WLR 212 (CA) is to adopt the following formula:-

(a) Assess in respect of each period of recovery the Deceased's net income and the dependent's net income. Add them together and allow two thirds of that joint net income (if the Deceased was married / in a civil partnership / cohabiting but without dependent children) or three quarters of that joint net income (if the Deceased was married / in a civil partnership / cohabiting but with dependent children).

(b) In respect of each such period subtract from that proportion of the joint net income the dependent's own net income.

That process undertaken according to *Harris* makes a conventional, and broad-brush, allowance for the sums which the Deceased would have been likely to have expended for his or her own personal benefit, rather than for the joint benefit of family finances.

The correct approach to multipliers, in respect of long-term periods of dependency, following Knauer v. Ministry of Justice [2016] AC 908 is to use the "*actuarially recommended approach*" provided for in paragraphs 128 – 160 of the Ogden Tables, 8th Edition (2020).

Loss of services dependency

Similarly, a loss of dependency upon valuable services can be claimed (such as DIY / Gardening / decorating / caring for a partner who is dependent upon care). This is valued according to how much it would cost to replace the lost service commercially or gratuitously (if the same is being or is to be replaced gratuitously), and assessing for how long the dependency would, but for the tort, have been provided for. This generally leads to a tapering of such claims towards the end of what would, but for the tort, have been the Deceased's natural life, to reflect the fact that the Deceased's ability to provide for the dependency would have diminished over time as his or her health would have been likely ultimately to begin to fail gradually.

Loss of partner or spouse

This is often claimed in a conventional, and relatively modest, sum of between about £2,500 and about £7,500. In principle it is probably legally irrecoverable if challenged:- Magill v. Panel Systems (DB) Ltd [2017] EWHC 1517 (QB) and Mosson v. Spousal (London) Limited [2016] EWHC 53 (QB).

PART THREE – ISSUES IN LIVING CLAIMS

(i) Introduction

Living claims present similar issues to any other type of injury claim where there are claims for special damage. The only real difference in asbestos-injury claims is that; firstly, they almost inevitably involve claims being calculated to the date of death since in the vast majority of cases, it will be the asbestos-related injury which either causes death or endures until death. Secondly, the period of loss is usually far shorter than would be the case in other types of injury cases sue to the aggressive nature of the injuries sustained once symptoms have begun to manifest – for reasons which we have discussed earlier in this book.

It ought to be noted that we do not cover loss of earnings, lost years claims or pension claims in this book in any great detail. Fundamentally, there is no reason why these can't be claimed where the onset of symptoms occurs whilst the Claimant is still working. However, given the latency period between exposure and symptom onset, it is uncommon for a Claimant still to be within the working phase of their life. The overwhelming majority of cases occur when Claimant's are in retirement and as such, no loss of earnings or pension contribution arises.

Regrettably though, one prominent factor to bear in mind in asbestos claims, is that generally speaking, living claims are worth less than fatal claims, since claims for dependency will often outweigh claims for future loss of earnings or lost years.

One area which is slightly peculiar to asbestos claims however, is the claims for future treatment costs. This will be the focus of section 3 of this part, below.

(ii) Financial losses to death

(a) Care and assistance

It is not unusual for there to be expert care / nursing evidence on this issue, generally from a Registered General Nurse (RGN). However, the real forensic benefit of such evidence is often that the nursing care expert gets to speak to the sufferer and his or her family during his or her lifetime. Where the sufferer has already died before that is possible it may be that solicitors can piece together, by way of factual evidence, the amount of care and assistance expended, rather than expert evidence on the issue being reasonably required.

There are broadly 2 types of care which is claimed:-

- Gratuitous care and assistance provided by family and friends of the Deceased.
- Commercially sourced care and assistance.

As to gratuitous care and assistance, the task is to determine how much time was spent providing care "*beyond the ordinary regime of family life*"[4] or "*beyond what a* [husband / wife] *would anyhow be doing for* [his or her] [husband / wife]"[5], by reason of the tort. That is then multiplied by an appropriate hourly rate, which is usually taken to be the appropriate rate for commercial care and assistance (the National Joint Council Payscales, spinal point 8 up to and including March 2019 and spinal pint 2 from April 2019 onwards) and reducing the same by a factor of 25% to reflect the gratuitous nature of the care and assistance alleged.

As to commercial care and assistance, this is usually proven by invoices showing the cost actually spent. The question then is one of whether or not the care obtained was reasonably required by reason of the tort.

---

4 Mills v. British Rail Engineering Limited [1992] PIQR Q130, at Q139, per Staughton LJ.

5 Giambrone v. Sunworld Holidays Limited [2004] PIQR Q4, per Brooke LJ, at [24].

(b) Loss of earnings, Pension Loss, and 'Lost Years' claims

In the case of a sufferer who was still in work when symptoms started and had to give up work prematurely by reason of the tort, the estate can in principle recover the net sums which the Deceased would have earned prior to death but for the tort and/or would have contributed to their later pension – the calculation is simply done on a traditional multiplier / multiplicand basis and by reference to the Ogden tables where appropriate.

The other type of claim normally advanced are a 'lost years' claim. It seems to have first been referred to in that way in the decision in Pickett v British Rail Engineering Limited [1980] AC 136. Lord Wilberforce said as follows[6]:

> *"My Lords, in the case of the adult wage earner with or without dependents who sues for damages during his lifetime, I am convinced that a rule which enables the "lost years" to be taken account of comes close to the ordinary man's expectations than one which limits his interest to his shortened span of life. The interest which such a man has in the earnings he might hope to make over a normal life, if not saleable in the market, has a value which can be assessed. A man who receives that assessed value would surely consider himself and be considered compensated – a man denied it would not".*

This element of claim seeks to claim for the income the Claimant would have received had he lived a 'normal' life absent the asbestos-related injury they now suffer. As such, it is only advanced in terminal illness claims where the Claimant is still alive. The Claimant will seek to evidence their life expectancy were it not for their illness, compared to their life expectancy with the illness, and claim for income they would have received in those years which have been 'lost'. That evidence will often require expertise on life expectancy and may also require accountancy input to determine the level of income. The amount yielded will then need to be discounted to reflect the proportion of receipts that the Claimant would have spent on themselves - custom-

6 Page 150(C)

arily the factor is normally 50%[7], but of course, it is relative to the level of income in a particular case[8] - and the net amount will be that which is recovered.

It is important to note though, that in making a lost years claim, the income which is the subject of that claim is that which is lost because of death – that must be distinguished from income which survives the Claimant's death and that proportion needs to be excluded from the claim – that point was made clear by HHJ Clarke in Head v The Culver Heating Co Limited [2019] EWHC 1217 (QB) at paragraph 66.

The net result though, is that because of the 50% discount generally applied to reflect costs of living which will not be expended due to death, a lost years claim is often worth less than a dependency claim which would be made in a fatal claim.

(c) Aids and equipment

It will not be unusual for aids and appliances, such as mobility scooters, stair lifts, adjustable beds, and smaller items to have been purchased in the lifetime of the Deceased to make life easier for the Deceased and / or his or her family by reason of the symptoms of the tort. It may be that further aids and equipment is required from the date of trial, and such future loss claims ought also to be recovered.

(d) Travel expenses

Reasonably travel expenses caused by the tort are recoverable. It is suggested that a log ought to be kept of individual journeys made to medical appointments and other appointments which have been occurred as a result of the injury sustained. The log should contain the date, destination, reason for the appointment and the number of miles

7 See Harris v Empress Motors [1984] 1 WLR 212

8 See Shanks v Swan Hunter Group PLC [2007] EWHC 1807 (QB)

incurred there and back. The rate normally applied is as per any type of case at £0.45 per mile.

(e) Medical expenses / subrogated medical insurance claims

The Deceased may have spent sums on his or her own treatment, or a private medical insurance may have expended sums on his or her behalf. If so, subject to proof of the expenses involved and such expenses being reasonable, they are recoverable. Claims for future expenses within this category can likewise be claimed.

(iii) Future Treatment Claims

In recent years there have been marked strides forward in the treatment of asbestos-induced tumours within the lungs and respiratory system, the most significant of which is known as immunotherapy. The 'front line' treatment for an asbestos-related tumour is often the same as with any form of cancer: chemotherapy. Immunotherapy, however, represents 'second line' treatment which is usually deployed after chemotherapy has been undertaken.

In late 2016 the National Institute for Health and Care Excellence (NICE) recommended that the NHS offer a new immunotherapy drug, pembrolizumab (also known as Keytruda) for routine use on the NHS for patients with advanced non-small cell lung cancer. In June 2018, the NHS announced that they would go with that recommendation.

The purpose of immunotherapy is to 'kick-start' the patient's immune system against cancerous cells – the drug does not directly target the tumour itself[9]. It therefore works differently to chemotherapy which does seek to directly attack cancer cells. Accordingly, one of the benefits of immunotherapy is that it is self-propagating if it is successful, with the immune system continuing to attack the tumour after the treatment

9 A useful overview of immunotherapy and how it works can be found here: https://www.asbestos.com/treatment/immunotherapy/

cycles have been completed. It was shown, in many trials, to benefit patients with non-small cell lung cancer, including mesothelioma (though the number of mesothelioma patients trialled were few). The main benefits shown in studies were longer life expectancy, and a reduction in the rate of tumour growth. In one study, the life expectancy increase was in the region of 16 months. The other benefit was that the side-effects of the treatment were generally less than those experienced by patients on a course of chemotherapy.

Over time, other immunotherapy drugs have also emerged; Nivolumab, Ipilimumab, Atezolizumab and Bevacizumab. All but Bevacizumab have become available on the NHS though qualification for them is required and is assessed on a case by case basis, and, importantly, no immunotherapy is available on the NHS to treat mesothelioma. Accordingly, the costs of such treatment will still be the subject of claims against Defendants for the foreseeable future.

The progression of these studies, and their measured success in mesothelioma patients, meant that they soon began to be featured on schedules of loss. The downside was the high costs of the treatment which had to be administered in cycles over a period of time – normally in the region of one cycle every 3 weeks. To paint that picture a little better, one course of treatment, in 2017, cost tens of thousands of pounds[10] and it was often regularly advised that there ought to be a minimum of around 3 courses on average, per patient but the treatment can take place over a period of up to 2 years. Of course, on the Defendant side, a difficult situation presented itself. On the one hand the trials had been far than conclusive as to the effectiveness of the drug in mesothelioma cases – there was therefore significant scepticism about how successful such treatment would be for those claiming it when compared to the cost. On the other hand, there was the potential for it to be successful and prolong a Claimant's life to some material degree.

Previous treatment of mesothelioma had been argued to be speculative and to be an unreasonable head of loss. That occurred in Najib v John Laing PLC [2011] EWHC 1016 (QB) when a Claimant made a past

10 Though costs of the treatment have now reduced to around £5,000 per course

loss claim for alternative treatment which he had sought to obtain to try and increase his life expectancy. The Claimant had undergone the treatment even though his treating physician had not recommended it or endorsed it. The Defendant sought to argue against its recovery at trial. Mrs Justice Nicola Davies held[11]:

> *"When the claimant's oncologist and general practitioner learnt of the proposed treatment, whatever their own reservations, they did not say "Do not undertake this treatment". The claimant, faced with a harsh, painful illness and a short life expectancy, was offered the chance of a longer life. He took it. I am unable to find that in these particular circumstances, the actions of the claimant were unreasonable. The actual cost of the treatment is high, but in the context of an extended life expectancy, it is not."*

The issue of immunotherapy in mesothelioma claims then came before the High Court in Hague v British Telecommunications PLC [2018] EWHC 2227. Master Thornett was asked to consider the extent to which a compromise agreement between the parties had caused the Defendant to become obliged to continue to fund private immunotherapy treatment. Discussing immunotherapy generally, Master Thornett said[12]:

> *"Immunotherapy is an innovative and new therapy that aims to stimulate the immune system to promote an anti-tumour immune effect rather than targeting the cancer cells themselves via drug treatment. However, no immunotherapy drugs have marked authorisation for use in mesothelioma either in the UK or elsewhere. There are currently no NICE guidelines that are relevant to the use of immunotherapy at any stage of therapy. Neither the British Thoracic Society nor the American Society for Clinical Oncology recommend immunotherapy for second line treatment of mesothelioma outside of clinical trials. There are few case studies available and these have to be interpreted with caution because of potential selection bias in the*

11 Para 20

12 Para 4

> *patients under review. The therapy remains within a rapidly evolving field."*

The Claimant had previously undergone chemotherapy in November 2017 with some success. It was therefore recommended that he undergo immunotherapy with Pembrolizumab in February 2018 and this commenced and four cycles were administered. By July 2018, the Claimants condition had begun to deteriorate and after seven cycles, the treatment was discontinued and the Claimant's treating doctor recommended switching to a combination of Ipilimumab and Nivolumab in order to achieve a prolonged life expectancy of around 4 months. The treatment was not available on the NHS and an estimated cost of over £21,000 was provided. In May 2018 however, the Claimant had compromised his claim against the Defendant. The agreement had recorded that the Defendant would pay any 'second line treatment' which was recommended by the Claimant's treating Oncologist.

The Defendant argued that the proposed new treatment was outside of the agreement as it was not envisaged at the time of the compromise when the Claimant was only being treated with Pembrolizumab. It was further argued that the Pembrolizumab course was 'second line treatment' after Chemotherapy and therefore the new treatment proposed was 'third line treatment' which was not part of the agreement. The Claimant contended that the 'new' treatment, was a continuation of the immunotherapy being given at the time of the agreement and it was therefore 'second line therapy' which had been described within the agreement as being something the Defendant would fund. The Judge agreed with the Claimant's arguments on this issue.

However, the compromise agreement also contained a 'reasonableness' clause in respect of the treatment. In that respect, the Claimant had to demonstrate that it was 'reasonable' for him to undertake the treatment proposed and the agreement required that any further treatment should be recommended by the Claimant's treating oncologist.

The Claimant's treating oncologist recommended the treatment. The Defendant adduced expert evidence that the treatment was not reasonable and therefore sought to challenge the view of the treating oncologist. In particular, they pointed to the lack of testing of immunotherapy treatments generally on mesothelioma patients and the fact that any successes which had occurred, had been related to the use of Pembrolizumab only. The Claimant's expert discussed his experience of two patients of his who had had similar treatment to that claimed by the Claimant which had had some success. Master Thornett, decided that the Claimant had, on balance, discharged the reasonableness burden. In so doing, he held[13]:

> *"This is a highly specialised area in which there is no NHS practice or NICE recognition. In this context, the fact Dr Szlosarek draws upon his personal experience within private medicine is to entirely be expected rather than constitute a point for implied adverse criticism. Anecdotal evidence may well be the lowest form of evidential hierarchy but does not, of itself, establish that clinical decisions drawn from it are therefore unreasonable. Indeed, were this the case it would lead to the remarkably concerning proposition that no medical practitioner could justify a decision unless based on peer reviewed clinical studies. Rationalised decisions based on personal clinical experience can surely still be justifiable and hence be reasonable providing any contraindications are not such that no other medical practitioner would consider them reasonable or be likely to take them."*

That then was the position in 2018. What is of note, is that since then, there have been no reported challenges before the Courts by Defendants as to the reasonableness of a future treatment claim for immunotherapy brought by a Claimant. The obvious question to ask, is why? The obvious answer is simply that Defendants have moved on from the argument and appear to be far more amenable to agreeing those types of claims provided that appropriately worded agreements as to how the treatment will be conducted can be made, and appropriate funding agreements for the treatments put in place. That latter aspect is something which we shall discuss in the next section. Of course, whether or not a Defendant in a particular case chooses in the future to take the

13 Para 46 (vi)

point again, remains to be seen, but for the present the position seems to have settled with both sides acknowledging that the treatment is an important issue for Claimants, generally, which ought to be dealt with by agreement rather than through the Courts. That point is best illustrated by the decision in Howard v The Imperial London Hotels Limited [2019] EWHC 202 (QB), which concerned a claim for future immunotherapy treatment, but where, instead of arguing whether it was a reasonable claim, the Defendant conceded the point and instead the Court and the parties focused on how the treatment should be funded.

Of course, in that same time frame, medical research as to the effectiveness of immunotherapy in treating asbestos-related tumours, and in particular, mesothelioma, has also continued. In February 2019, the Mesothelioma Stratified Therapy trial (MiST) launched with funding from the British Lung Foundation. That trial is continuing at the time of writing. In addition, Cancer Research UK launched a trial looking specifically at the treatment of mesothelioma with Nivolumab. The recruitment for that trial – which aimed to recruit 336 participants - ceased in March 2020 and their findings are awaited[14].

The following can then be adduced about future treatment claims in asbestos cases:

- Firstly, there is a profound human dimension to such claims. It takes bold arguments, and perhaps even bolder judges, to deprive a Claimant of the opportunity of prolonging their life.

- Secondly, as the science and clinical testing continues to evolve, so too will this type of claim. It is fair to say that the scientific rationale for immunotherapy is still evolving and it is certainly not clear-cut.

- From a Defendant's perspective, though claims initially represented risk both in terms of cost/benefit, and issues of

14 Further information can be found at https://www.cancerresearchuk.org/about-cancer/find-a-clinical-trial/a-trial-looking-at-nivolumab-for-mesothelioma-confirm#undefined

reasonableness, there does seem to have been a shift forwards towards finding ways of ensuring the treatment is accessible to Claimants though at the same time acceptably defined as to its extent and the way that it will be funded. As such, it seems unlikely, at this juncture, that any further disputes as to the reasonableness of future immunotherapy treatment, will be had.

- Compromise agreements will therefore need to carefully consider the point. Of course, it very much depends on the Claimant and the progression of their condition. Some will be simply too far gone for the treatment to be viable. But for those for whom it is viable, exactly what treatment is to be given, and how, is something which needs to be carefully recorded and agreed.
- Where there is a compromise agreement it is common for the decision on future treatment to be something which must be recommended and supported by the Claimant's treating oncologist (as was the case in *Hague*). That is likely to still be a position which remains and guides the nature of this type of claim going forward.
- The other relevant issue is how the treatment ought to be funded. That is something that we will look at in the next section of this chapter.

(iv) Payment of Future Damages in Living Claims

Another issue which arises in living claims is how the future damages ought to be paid in respect of certain heads of loss where there is uncertainty due to the Claimant's prognosis or a short life expectancy. In short, there is a concern that some items of loss, though reasonably claimed, will never in fact be incurred and therefore the Claimant's estate could receive a windfall in respect of monies left over, or where the future is just so uncertain that any order is difficult to word without risking the need to have its terms adjudicated on again by a Court.

The most obvious example, is the future treatment claims which we have just looked at – where, for example, a Claimant claims the future costs of immunotherapy but his condition could deteriorate before it finishes thus making it no longer viable. A Defendant will inevitably be concerned as to what happens to any damages which went unspent and an order as to when such damages ought to be paid will also be difficult because the treatment is indefinite.

Generally, there are four ways in which parties can bridge the gap between ensuring the Claimant is properly compensated whilst also avoiding any windfall for damages received but which are not then incurred. They are:

- Periodical Payment Orders (PPO's) – under Section 2(1) of the Damages Act 1996 and further to CPR 41.17.
- Reversionary Trusts – whereby damages are placed into a trust fund to he drawn down as and when required by the Claimant but with the Defendant retaining a reversionary interest in any sums not drawn down.
- Interim payments – made by application as and when required, to the Court via Part 23 Notices.
- Agreements negotiated between the parties.

As to which methodology was generally preferable in the context of asbestos claims, Master Thornett outlined guidance in Howard v The Imperial London Hotels Limited [2019] EWHC 202 (QB). The claim in question concerned the claim for future immunotherapy treatment. There was no issue that the Claimant ought to recover the costs of such treatment, but the Claimant sought to have such damages paid by way of a PPO. The Defendant was concerned that there was insufficient certainty that would allow for a PPO to be used. Master Thornett agreed with the Defendant on that issue[15]:

15 Para 11

"a PPO following exclusively the format of the legislation and CPR 41.8 is obliged to award an annual amount paid by way of a regular payment when neither can be said to reflect the anticipated future with very much accuracy. The Claimant observes that element of future uncertainty by way of need is, of course, present in any PPO. The feature of using a PPO in the case of immunotherapy, however, would at its very commencement be (a) entirely speculative in the case of a claimant not currently in receipt of immunotherapy (b) in the case of a claimant currently in receipt of immunotherapy, be based on a clinical status quo of uncertain duration and justification."

Likewise, the establishment of a trust was also rejected since the costs and administration of setting up that trust are often going to be disproportionate to the length of time for which it is needed in cases of asbestos injury where life expectancy will, inevitably, be short[16].

The Court therefore opted for interim payments as being the most appropriate mechanism in such circumstances[17]:

"I am satisfied that drawing upon interim payments to fund immunotherapy in the circumstances of a case such as this, where the Claimant's life expectancy is very limited, is by far the more flexible and appropriate tool than a PPO. My reasons focus not only upon practical advantages and disadvantages featured in respectively the two mechanisms but also factors in the considerable procedural flexibility and (I believe) efficiency afforded to parties bringing and defending claims in the Asbestos List and as would immediately apply to any interim payment application. This second observation substantially informs and eclipses any process of comparing and contrasting the two mechanisms."

Accordingly, interim payment applications where deemed to be preferable in such circumstances. In doing so, the Court backed the Judge led procedure which deals with asbestos claims – something

16 See Para 48

17 Para 38

which we will turn to in the next Chapter – to provide the degree of urgency required to facilitate those applications without delay.

(v) Provisional Damages applications

Applications for provisional damages are commonplace in living asbestos-related injury claims. They are made by Claimants to ensure that they have some early payment of damages which they can use to fund ongoing treatment or improve their quality of life where their life expectancy is short or uncertain.

The power to award provisional damages comes from section 51 of the County Courts Act 1984 and section 32A of the Supreme Court Act 1981. Section 32A of the SCA 1981 states:

> *"(1) This section applies to an action for damages for personal injuries in which there is proved or admitted to be a chance that at some definite or indefinite time in the future the injured person will, as a result of the act or omission which gave rise to the cause of action, develop some serious disease or suffer some serious deterioration in his physical or mental condition.*
>
> *(2) Subject to subsection (4) below, as regards any action for damages to which this section applies in which a judgment is given in the High Court, provision may be made by rules of court for enabling the court, in such circumstances as may be prescribed, to award the injured person—*
>
> *(a) damages assessed on the assumption that the injured person will not develop the disease or suffer the deterioration in his condition; and*
>
> *(b) further damages at a future date if he develops the disease or suffers the deterioration."*

The award is, however, only capable of being granted where the Claimant demonstrates that there is a real chance that their condition will deteriorate at some point in the future, and before they will likely receive full settlement or award from the Court[18]. Even once those conditions are fulfilled, the award is still discretionary. However, in cases of mesothelioma, for example, the threshold test is unlikely to be a high hurdle to a Claimant. The test was set out in XX v Whittington Hospital NHS Trust [2017] EWHC 2318 (QB) by Sir Robert Nelson[19]:

> *"The test for determining whether an award of provisional damages is appropriate is threefold. Firstly whether the risk of deterioration is real rather than fanciful, secondly whether the deterioration will be serious, and thirdly whether the case is a proper one in which to depart from the normal rule of awarding damages on a once and for all basis at the date of trial. The court is exercising its discretion in considering the test and must take into account in doing so the likely clarity of any future risk and the ease with which it can be separated from the existing medical condition. (Wilson v Ministry of Defence (1991) 1 AER 638, Kotula v EDF (2011) EWHC1546 QB, Yale-Helms v Countess of Chester Hospital NHS Foundation Trust Lawtel 10 November 2015, Curi v Colina The Times 14 October 1998.)*
>
> *30. Applying those tests to these facts I am clear that the risk of deterioration at 30 – 40% even though it only arises if the surrogacy fails, is real rather than fanciful. The second limb of the test presents a more difficult problem. It is difficult, in my judgement, to hold that a deterioration which may be severe but which is likely to be temporary and treated successfully in about one year can properly be regarded as serious under the test for provisional damages. This is not one of those rare cases where the normal rules for the awarding of damages should be displaced. The Claimant can be properly compensated within the normal rules. There is also the problem, which may arise, of establishing the origins of a particular psychological condition or its exacerbation. It is not therefore an appropriate case in which I should exercise my discretion in favour of an award of provisional damages regarding psychological injury."*

18 See Scott Baker J in Wilson v Ministry of Defence [1991] 1 All ER 638 at 642B

19 Paragraphs 29 – 30

CPR 41 sets out the requirement that any such application for provisional damages must be referred to within the Particulars of Claim – that is a mandatory requirement – and outline the grounds upon which the award is required[20].

A peculiar aspect of such applications is the issue of causation. At the time that the application is made, the Claimant need not demonstrate a causal link between the condition which will become the subject of the claim, and the wrongdoing on the Defendant. This is plainly beneficial in asbestos claims since material contribution is likely to be an issue of some controversy until expert evidence is obtained from hygienists and medics, and that is evidence which is unlikely to be available and settled at the commencement of the claim. Those issues are reserved for trial.

The contents of the Order for Provisional Damages are set out at CPR 41.2(2).

Another issue is what happens if the deterioration does materialise after a provisional award is made, and the Claimant succumbs to that deterioration. In such cases, the deceased's estate may still wish to pursue a claim under the Fatal Accidents Act 1976. Section 3 of the Damages Act 1996 makes it plain that that is permissible and that any award of provisional damages should not de-bar that future claim from being brought by the estate:

> *"(2) The award of the provisional damages shall not operate as a bar to an action in respect of that person's death under the M1Fatal Accidents Act 1976.*
>
> *(3) Such part (if any) of—*
>
> *(a) the provisional damages; and*
>
> *(b) any further damages awarded to the person in question before his death,*

20 CPR 16.4(1)(d) and 16PD 4.4(1)

> *as was intended to compensate him for pecuniary loss in a period which in the event falls after his death shall be taken into account in assessing the amount of any loss of support suffered by the person or persons for whose benefit the action under the Fatal Accidents Act 1976 is brought."*

Accordingly, the provisional award will not bar a future claim, but any sums made under it may be set-off against any damages received for like heads of loss successfully made by the estate.

CHAPTER NINE
PROCEDURE

(i) Introduction

Asbestos litigation has attracted special procedural rules which ought to be used by parties. The reasoning behind these is the specialist nature of asbestos litigation generally, combined with the recognised need to try and fast track claims as expeditiously as possible where the Claimant is still alive and therefore the resolution of the claim is likely to allow some improved quality of life. Initially, the process existed for those Claimant's suffering from mesothelioma – the procedure thereafter became known as the 'mesothelioma list'. However, since then it has gone on to become incorporated within Practice Direction 3D of the CPR and its success of ensuring flexibility and speed wherever possible, has caused it to be used in all types of asbestos-related injury claims.

In order to properly effect the special procedure, there was a recognised need to ensure that claims are dealt with by Judges who are familiar and experienced with all aspects of asbestos litigation, hence the so-called 'Masters Corridor' at the Royal Courts of Justice sitting within the Queen's Bench Division, which houses the majority of judges who will deal, at least in terms of case management, with asbestos claims coming through. Indeed, the procedure was, initially, Judge-made being created by the then Senior Master, Master Whitaker. The number of Masters has since increased over time (there are presently five) and they are supported by Deputies where needed, but the core aims of encouraging a flexible and efficient approach to litigation, has remained. Each Master now also has their own designated clerk to act as a first point of contact for urgent requests from parties which enable faster listing and judicial attention.

Accordingly, it is necessary for any litigator involved in asbestos litigation, to familiarise themselves with the proper procedure to be adopted and its requirements.

(ii) The genesis of the procedure

A really very useful starting point is the overview of the procedure which was given by Master McCloud in Yates v Commissioners for Her Majesty's Revenue & Customs [2014] EWHC 2311 (QB). That case arose as a result of an in issue which arose in respect of obtaining a Claimant's employment history from HMRC tax returns. However, the Court nonetheless took the opportunity to outline the asbestos claims procedure and history.

In her judgment, Master McCloud emphasised the overarching realities of asbestos litigation in paragraph 16 of her judgment:

> *"Each delay in a living asbestos claim has a penalty associated with it which is measurable as a proportion of the claimants in the system who will die without a claim being dealt with during that delay. Weeks lost imply lives ended without resolution of the claim, and that can also mean lost evidence which could have assisted either party. Yet where there is a properly arguable defence with a real prospect of success, the Defendant is entitled to a trial and it would be a serious injustice to a Defendant to deny it that right merely so as to ensure speedy hearing of claims, despite the often inevitable consequence that the Claimant will pass away before trial."*

Accordingly, the procedure was designed to be:

- Flexible
- Capable of being swiftly administered by specialist Masters
- Informal wherever possible
- Sensitive to the needs of the parties

The over-arching benefits were that the Masters could be contacted directly by the parties where there were issues, and there could also therefore be more time and cost-efficiencies with a view to ensuring that, in particular, the Claimant's evidence is properly preserved.

To allow for proper and efficient judicial referral of applications and other issues which arise, there is a special email address available to parties to enable matters to be urgently referred to the Masters:

qb.asbestos@justice.gov.uk

(iii) The Pre-Action Protocol for Industrial Disease Claims

The first point to make is that each asbestos claim is subject to the overall pre-action protocol for industrial disease claims. The only exception being those claims which involve a Claimant who is still alive but suffering with mesothelioma. For those types of claims, there are further provisions and requirements outlined in Practice Direction 3D which applies specifically to Mesothelioma claims, and which builds upon the RCJ Masters procedure which we have just looked at.

It is beyond the scope of this work to look at the pre-action protocol for ID claims in any great detail. However, it will be noted that in asbestos claims, there is more flexibility and expected efficiency with matters being dealt with on a more urgent basis.

(iv) Practice Direction 3D

CPR PD 3D is a very important starting point for asbestos-related injury claims. Though entitled 'Mesothelioma Claims', its application has been more general across all aspects of asbestos injury claims and as such, is more often than not employed by parties, and adhered to, in the majority of asbestos claims.

The crucial elements of what is required, are:

- The Claim Form and Particulars of Claim must state on them whether the claim is 'Fatal' or 'Living': Para 3.1;
- To be attached to the Claim Form is the Claimant's HMRC Schedule and the initial Letter of Claim: para 3.4;

- Once issued and the procedure incepted, the first issue to be determined is whether or not the Defendant can 'show cause' to defend the claim on the issue of breach of duty. That will often be the subject of the first CMC: para 3.2;
- Accordingly, there will be a need for the filing of early witness statements and evidence by the parties on the issue of liability;
- The contents of the liability witness statements are then referred to in para 3.3;
- Where the Claimant has limited life expectancy, the Court needs to be made aware of that fact and the reasons why: para 4;
- Appropriate directions will then be made moving forward to trial.

(a) The Show Cause Procedure

The 'show cause' procedure is the first watershed moment in any asbestos claim. It is an important part of the case which dictates the shape of the litigation thereafter and the procedure is unique to asbestos claims. A failure by a Defendant to show cause as to why they ought to be permitted to defend the claim will result in judgment being entered against them at that first hearing - either on the claim as a whole, or on an isolated issue such as breach. Paragraph 6 of the Practice Direction is dedicated to the procedure and what is expected.

Paragraph 6.1 of the Practice Direction specifically denies the process as thus:

> *"The show cause procedure is a requirement by the court, of its own initiative and usually on a 'costs in the case' basis, for the Defendant to evidence and legal arguments that give the defendant a real prospect of success on any or all issues of liability."*

In HM Revenue & Customs v Silcock [2009] EWHC 3025 Mr Justice Sweeney elaborated somewhat on that outline of the procedure[1]:

> *"At a show cause hearing it is for the Claimant to adduce credible evidence in support of his case, and it is only if he does so that the Defendant becomes subject to an evidential burden to show cause. It is further agreed that the correct test is not whether the Defendant's case is likely to succeed at trial, but only whether it has some chance of success and the prospects are not fanciful.*
>
> *"It follows that at a show cause hearing, it is open to a Defendant to submit that the Claimant's evidence is such as to mean that the Claimant is unlikely to succeed, and thus that the Defendant has shown cause that he has a realistic prospect of success. Further or in the alternative, the Defendant may make submissions based on evidence which he has served. Obviously if the former course alone is chosen, the Defendant must bear the risk of having no evidence of his own to determine any appropriate inferences to be drawn from the Claimant's evidence."*

The burden of proof, therefore, remains on the Claimant initially – the procedure does not reverse that position from the outset – the Claimant must still discharge an initial evidential burden as to the crucial components of the claim. Thereafter, the procedure flips the burden onto the Defendant to show that they have a real prospect of defending the claim - the test is akin to that for summary judgment and therefore the line authority application to that test is relevant here – see for example ED & F Mann Liquid Products v Patel [2003] EWCA Civ 472. The test was recently summarised in the decision of Mr Justice Turner in Helm v William Kenyon & Sons Ltd & Somewatch Limited [2019] EWHC 1108 (QB), at paragraph 4:

> *"The show cause is aimed at identifying promptly those defences that have no real prospect of success. In formal terms, the obligation remains on the claimant throughout the presentation of credible*

1 Paras 9 and 10

evidence to establish a prima facie case following which an evidential burden then shifts to the defendant to demonstrate, notwithstanding, that there are reasonable prospects of success. In that context, 'reasonable' means more than merely fanciful."

The streamlined nature of the process plainly allows for some rough justice in terms of the way in which evidence is properly tested, but the rationale for the procedure makes it plainly justified. It was estimated in Helm that the procedure is thought to identify approximately 95% of Defendants as having no real prospect of success[2].

Of course, it is even more difficult for cases involving a single Defendant, particularly in cases of mesothelioma. This was discussed in obiter by Mr Justice Turner in Helm, at paragraph 17:

"It is tempting, in cases in which there is only one defendant and only one potential employment when the claimant is exposed to asbestos, to work backwards from the established fact that mesothelioma, by and large, is overwhelmingly (not exclusively) caused by exposure to asbestos. So if there is only one defendant, then it equips the judge to say with relative confidence, all other things being equal, that there was exposure and that it is very likely, in those circumstances, that the claimant will establish liability."

Issues concerning causation will also be debated at the hearing and subjected to the same test – the analysis is not confined to breach of duty, though the ultimate decision may be. Plainly though, a Defendant will need to show credible medical evidence to rebut any diagnosis made by the Claimant's expert.

In attempting to show cause, the principal arguments centre on the credibility and reliability of the Claimant's evidence and whether that sufficiently discharges the initial evidential burden upon them, adducing rebuttal evidence (either documentary, from a witness or from an expert) to the Claimant's allegations on exposure, or demonstrating

2 Per Mr Justice Turner at paragraph 17

some other reason why a trial is necessary (limitation for example, or causation evidence). Accordingly, it is imperative that evidence is obtained and filed in advance of that first CMC – a Defendant who comes to the hearing with no evidence and only speculation is likely to be given short shrift by the Masters – particularly when they were served with a letter of claim years beforehand.

The Court then has the following options:

- Enter judgment for the Claimant on the whole of the claim with damages to be assessed;
- Find for the Claimant on an isolated issue (i.e. breach) and direct a trial on the remaining issues; or
- Hold that the Defendant has shown cause and give directions to an all issues trial.

Due to the fact that the show cause hearing is a requirement of the Practice Direction and is a hearing of the Court's own motion, the usual costs order – regardless of outcome, is costs in the case.

(b) Evidence on Deposition

Another common feature in asbestos claims is a requirement for evidence on deposition. By in large, it is the Claimant who gives their evidence on deposition – this is particularly so in those claims where the Claimant's life expectancy is especially short and there is a real risk that they will not live to trial. Of course, it can apply to any material witness, however. In short, it is imperative that the Court preserves as much evidence as it can so that a proper, and fair trial, can be held.

Where such evidence is to be taken by deposition, the Practice Direction deals with it under paragraph 8. That makes it clear that any such application ought to be made as soon as possible, and normally, by no later point than the first CMC and it will generally be regarded as a good reason to adjourn that CMC and the issue of showing cause until after that evidence has been taken.

However, though common in asbestos claims, such applications are not granted simply as routine. A Defendant must demonstrate the reasons why the Claimant needs to be cross-examined. An order for evidence on deposition from a Claimant will not be granted merely to give the Defendant an opportunity to look for a defence – it must be being done to further a defence. For that reason, it is highly unusual for evidence on deposition to be ordered in a case where a Defendant has not shown cause.

In terms of the process, the parties will always have to work closely in making the appropriate arrangements. The guiding rule of procedure is however Part 34 of the CPR, particularly CPR 34.8 and 34.11. In short order, the fundamentals are:

- The time, date and place must be agreed having regard to the witnesses needs.
- The deposition must be recorded on a DVD which is capable of being played in Court.
- A transcript of the evidence ought to be obtained and ought to feature in any subsequent trial bundle.
- An examiner of the Court ought to be appointed – note that it will not normally be a judge who oversees the deposition.
- There needs to be a statement or witness summary provided in advance of the deposition from the witness in question.
- There should then be a full opportunity for cross-examination of the witness.

If the evidence obtained by deposition is then wished to be relied upon by a party at trial (or subsequent show cause hearing), they must notify the other side and the Court of that intention. That is a mandatory requirement of CPR 34.11(2) and the time limit for doing so is at least 21 days prior to the trial[3]. It should be noted that a party is not obliged to use the evidence, it is their choice. In any event though, once obtained, the evidence becomes a disclosable document which any other party has a right to inspect – regardless of whether or not it is to be relied upon by the party who obtained it. Any deposed evidence which is then relied upon at trial, is afforded the same evidential status of a witness statement[4]. In some cases, there is the potential for a party to apply to the court for the witness whose evidence was given on deposition, to attend trial for further examination. That is possible under CPR 34.11(4) but it is noted that this can only be done where practicable and indeed, the commentary makes it clear that it would be "highly unusual"[5] for the Court to make such an order.

(v) Conclusion

It is hoped that that provides a succinct summary of the crucial aspects of procedure which affect asbestos claims. Of course, there are other more general requirements which also apply – particularly, and most notably, in respect of funding[6] and costs budgeting but those are beyond the scope of this book.

Overall, though, it is hoped that, if nothing else, the importance co-operation and dialogue between the parties and the Court has been suitably emphasised to achieve the desirable aims of efficient and expeditious litigation of these claims.

---

3 CPR 34.11(3)

4 CPR 34.11(5)

5 Commentary at 34.11.1

6 Specifically, it ought to be noted that section 44 – 46 of the Legal Aid, Sentencing and Punishment of Offenders Act 2012 do not apply to mesothelioma claims by virtue of section 48 of the same Act

CHAPTER TEN
LIMITATION DEFENCES

(i) Introduction

This chapter will address limitation in both living and fatal claims. The first question in either case is whether or not the claim is within time under Sections 11 or 12 of the Limitation Act 1980 and, if it is not, whether or not the Court should exercise its discretion under Section 33 of the 1980 Act to disapply the primary limitation period.

Due to the speed with which mesothelioma attacks the body and causes death, it is relatively rare for there to be an arguable issue about limitation, because the claim is usually brought within the primary limitation period. It can, however, happen, particularly in a fatal case. The issue is generally, however, much more common in the other asbestos claims. The principles, if the issue does arise, are, however, in any event, the same.

(ii) Living claims

(a) The proper order in which issues should be considered

As is not uncommon, if limitation is tried alongside the substantive issues in a case, it is important "*not to put the cart before the horse*". The Court should, when ruling upon the case, consider limitation first, and should not determine the substantive issues before determining the issue of limitation. As Auld LJ explained in paragraph 74 of KR v. Bryn Alyn Community (Holdings) Limited [2003] QB 1441:-

> "*(vii) Where a judge determines the section 33 issue along with the substantive issues in the case, he should take care not to determine the substantive issues, including liability, causation and quantum, before determining the issue of limitation and, in particular, the effect of delay on the cogency of the evidence. Much of such evidence, by*

reason of the lapse of time, may have been incapable of being adequately tested or contradicted before him. To rely on his findings on those issues to assess the cogency of the evidence for the purpose of the limitation exercise would put the cart before the horse. Put another way, it would effectively require a defendant to prove a negative, namely, that the judge could not have found against him on one or more of the substantive issues if he had tried the matter earlier and without the evidential disadvantages resulting from delay.

(viii) Where a judge has assessed the likely cogency of the available evidence, that is, before finding either way on the substantive issues in the case, he should keep in mind in balancing the respective prejudice to the parties that the more cogent the claimant's case the greater the prejudice to the defendant in depriving him of the benefit of the limitation period. As Parker LJ showed in Hartley v Birmingham City District Council [1992] 1 WLR 968, 979, such a finding is usually neutral on the balance of prejudice:

"in all, or nearly all, cases the prejudice to the plaintiff by the operation of the relevant limitation provision and the prejudice which would result to the defendant if the relevant provision were disapplied will be equal and opposite. The stronger the plaintiff's case the greater is the prejudice to him from the operation of the provision and the greater will be the prejudice to the defendant if the provision is disapplied ... as the prejudice resulting from the loss of the limitation defence will always or almost always be balanced by the prejudice to the plaintiff from the operation of the limitation provision the loss of the defence as such *will be of little importance. What is of paramount importance is the effect of the delay on the defendant's ability to defend."*

(b) The time within which the claim should be brought

Section 11 of the 1980 Act provides materially as follows:-

“***11 Special time limit for actions in respect of personal injuries.***

> ...
>
> *(3) An action to which this section applies shall not be brought after the expiration of the period applicable in accordance with subsection (4) or (5) below.*
>
> *(4) Except where subsection (5) below applies, the period applicable is three years from—*
>
> *(a) the date on which the cause of action accrued; or*
>
> *(b) the date of knowledge (if later) of the person injured*".

As to accrual of the cause of action, this is not before actionable injury or loss, in the sense of more than "*de minimis*" injury has been suffered. So, unless and until changes occur in the body which constitute a more than "*de minimis*" injury can the time start to run. So, the development of pleural plaques will not start the limitation clock running, because those are "*de minimis*" only.

If later than the date of accrual of the cause of action, the Claimant may rely upon the "*date of knowledge*". In this regard, Section 14 of the 1980 Act provides materially as follows:-

> *"14 Definition of date of knowledge for purposes of sections 11 and 12.*
>
> *(1) … in sections 11 and 12 of this Act references to a person's date of knowledge are references to the date on which he first had knowledge of the following facts—*
>
> *(a) that the injury in question was significant; and*
>
> *(b) that the injury was attributable in whole or in part to the act or omission which is alleged to constitute negligence, nuisance or breach of duty; and*
>
> *(c) the identity of the defendant; and*

> *(d) if it is alleged that the act or omission was that of a person other than the defendant, the identity of that person and the additional facts supporting the bringing of an action against the defendant;*
>
> *and knowledge that any acts or omissions did or did not, as a matter of law, involve negligence, nuisance or breach of duty is irrelevant.*
>
> *(2) For the purposes of this section an injury is significant if the person whose date of knowledge is in question would reasonably have considered it sufficiently serious to justify his instituting proceedings for damages against a defendant who did not dispute liability and was able to satisfy a judgment.*
>
> *(3) For the purposes of this section a person's knowledge includes knowledge which he might reasonably have been expected to acquire —*
>
> *(a) from facts observable or ascertainable by him; or*
>
> *(b) from facts ascertainable by him with the help of medical or other appropriate expert advice which it is reasonable for him to seek;*
>
> *but a person shall not be fixed under this subsection with knowledge of a fact ascertainable only with the help of expert advice so long as he has taken all reasonable steps to obtain (and, where appropriate, to act on) that advice".*

As to the burden of proof on the issue of whether or not the claim is in time or not, as Purchas LJ noted in Nash v. Eli Lilly & Co. [1993] 1 WLR 782 at 796H:-

> *"finally it is important to remember where the onus of proof lies. H If the writ is not issued within three years of the date when the cause of action arose (section ll(4)(a)), the onus is on the plaintiff to plead and prove a date within the three years preceding the date of the issue of the writ (section ll(4)(fc)). If the defendant wishes to rely on a date prior to the three year period immediately preceding the issue of the*

> *writ, the onus is on the defendant to prove that the plaintiff had or ought to have had knowledge by that date*".

As Hickinbottom J, as he then was, explained in Summers v. City and County of Cardiff [2015] EWHC 3066 (QB) (a diffuse pleural thickening claim), at sub-paragraph 10(iii):

> "*the test for "significance" of injury is one of quantum alone, and does not invite consideration of the cause or nature of the injury (Dobbie at page 1241H). But, for an injury to be "significant" for these purposes, the quantum level is low: it has been said that the test comes close to the test of seriousness of an injury for which the courts could properly award damages and thus in respect of which a cause of action in negligence accrues(Cartledge v E Jopling & Sons Limited [1963] AC 758 at 781; Rothwell v Chemical & Insulating Company Limited [2006] EWCA Civ 27; [2006] ICR 1458 at [21]). That test is essentially an illustration of the principle "de minimis non curat lex". Thus, where an injury is any more than very minor, it will generally satisfy the test for "significance" in section 14(2)*".

The test is an objective one, and not one of whether the Claimant himself, subjectively, considered the injury to be significant. Please see paragraph 34 of A v. Hoare [2008] 1 AC 844, per Lord Hoffmann:-

> "*Section 14(2) is a test for what counts as a significant injury. The material to which that test applies is generally "subjective" in the sense that it is applied to what the claimant knows of his injury rather than the injury as it actually was. Even then, his knowledge may have to be supplemented with imputed "objective" knowledge under Section 14(3). But the test itself is an entirely impersonal standard: not whether the claimant himself would have considered the injury sufficiently serious to justify proceedings but whether he would "reasonably" have done so. You ask what the claimant knew about the injury he had suffered, you add any knowledge about the injury which may be imputed to him under Section 14(3) and you then ask whether a reasonable person with that knowledge would*

> *have considered the injury sufficiently serious to justify his instituting proceedings for damages against a defendant who did not dispute liability and was able to satisfy a judgment*".

As to what is required for knowledge that an injury is attributable to occupational exposure, please see Spargo v. North Essex District Health Authority [1997] PIQR 235 at 242 per Brooke LJ.

> "*(1) The knowledge required to satisfy section 14(1)(b) is a broad knowledge of the essence of the causally relevant act or omission to which the injury is attributable;*
>
> *(2) "Attributable" in this context means "capable of being attributed to", in the sense of being a real possibility;*
>
> *(3) A plaintiff has the requisite knowledge when she knows enough to make it reasonable for her to begin to investigate whether or not she has a case against the defendant. Another way of putting this is to say that she will have such knowledge if she so firmly believes that her condition is capable of being attributed to an act or omission which she can identify (in broad terms) that she goes to a solicitor to seek advice about making a claim for compensation*".

Drawing these matters together, Laing J, stated in Lloyd v. Humphreys & Glasgow Limited [2015] EWHC (QB)[1] that "*It follows that once a claimant who has been negligently exposed to asbestos develops a significant injury (such as asbestosis, diffuse pleural thickening, or symptomatic pleural plaques), he has a cause of action. Time starts to run for the purposes of section 11. It is common ground that he has a separate cause of action against each defendant (if there are more than one) who has negligently exposed him to asbestos. The point when he knows (or ought reasonably to have found out) that he has a significant injury, and who exposed him to asbestos, is his date of knowledge for the purposes of section 14*".

1 Paragraph 89

(c) Section 33

If the claim is out of time, the Court has a discretion under Section 33 to permit the claim to proceed:-

> *"33 Discretionary exclusion of time limit for actions in respect of personal injuries or death.*
>
> *(1) If it appears to the court that it would be equitable to allow an action to proceed having regard to the degree to which— (a) the provisions of section 11 … of this Act prejudice the plaintiff or any person whom he represents; and (b) any decision of the court under this subsection would prejudice the defendant or any person whom he represents; the court may direct that those provisions shall not apply to the action, or shall not apply to any specified cause of action to which the action relates.*
>
> …
>
> *(3) In acting under this section the court shall have regard to all the circumstances of the case and in particular to—*
>
> *(a) the length of, and the reasons for, the delay on the part of the plaintiff;*
>
> *(b) the extent to which, having regard to the delay, the evidence adduced or likely to be adduced by the plaintiff or the defendant is or is likely to be less cogent than if the action had been brought within the time allowed by section 11 [F4, by section 11A] or (as the case may be) by section 12;*
>
> *(c) the conduct of the defendant after the cause of action arose, including the extent (if any) to which he responded to requests reasonably made by the plaintiff for information or inspection for the purpose of ascertaining facts which were or might be relevant to the plaintiff's cause of action against the defendant;*

(d) the duration of any disability of the plaintiff arising after the date of the accrual of the cause of action;

(e) the extent to which the plaintiff acted promptly and reasonably once he knew whether or not the act or omission of the defendant, to which the injury was attributable, might be capable at that time of giving rise to an action for damages;

(f) the steps, if any, taken by the plaintiff to obtain medical, legal or other expert advice and the nature of any such advice he may have received".

On 1 December 2017 the Court of Appeal summarised the principles to be applied under Section 33 in Chief Constable of Greater Manchester Police v. Carroll [2017] EWCA Civ 1992 at sub-paragraphs 42(1) – (12):-

"*42. Section 33(3) of LA 1980 requires the court, when exercising its discretion under section 33(1), to have regard to all the circumstances of the case but also directs the court to have regard to the five matters specified in sub-sections 33(3)(a)-(f). There are numerous reported cases in which the court has elaborated on the application of that statutory direction in the context of the particular facts of the case. In many of the cases the court has stated various principles of general application. The general principles may be summarised as follows.*

1) Section 33 is not confined to a "residual class of cases". It is unfettered and requires the judge to look at the matter broadly: Donovan v Gwentoys Ltd [1990] 1 WLR 472 at 477E; Horton v Sadler [2006] UKHL 27, [2007] 1 AC 307, at [9] (approving the Court of Appeal judgments in Finch v Francis unrptd 21.7.1977); A v Hoare [2008] UKHL 6, [2008] 1 AC 844, at [45], [49], [68] and [84]; Sayers v Lord Chelwood [2012] EWCA Civ 1715 [2013] 1 WLR 1695, at [55].

2) The matters specified in section 33(3) are not intended to place a fetter on the discretion given by section 33(1), as is made plain by the opening words "the court shall have regard to all the circumstances of the case", but to focus the attention of the court on matters which past experience has shown are likely to call for evaluation in the exercise of the discretion and must be taken into a consideration by the judge: Donovan at 477H-478A.

3) The essence of the proper exercise of the judicial discretion under section 33 is that the test is a balance of prejudice and the burden is on the claimant to show that his or her prejudice would outweigh that to the defendant: Donovan at 477E; Adams v Bracknell Forest Borough Council [2004] UKHL 29, [2005] 1 AC 76, at [55], approving observations in Robinson v St. Helens Metropolitan Borough Council [2003] PIQR P9 at [32] and [33]; McGhie v British Telecommunications plc [2005] EWCA Civ 48, (2005) 149 SJLB 114, at [45]. Refusing to exercise the discretion in favour of a claimant who brings the claim outside the primary limitation period will necessarily prejudice the claimant, who thereby loses the chance of establishing the claim.

4) The burden on the claimant under section 33 is not necessarily a heavy one. How heavy or easy it is for the claimant to discharge the burden will depend on the facts of the particular case: Sayers at [55].

5) Furthermore, while the ultimate burden is on a claimant to show that it would be inequitable to disapply the statute, the evidential burden of showing that the evidence adduced, or likely to be adduced, by the defendant is, or is likely to be, less cogent because of the delay is on the defendant: Burgin v Sheffield City Council [2015] EWCA Civ 482 at [23]. If relevant or potentially relevant documentation has been destroyed or lost by the defendant irresponsibly, that is a factor which may weigh against the defendant: Hammond v West Lancashire Health Authority [1998] Lloyd's Rep Med 146.

6) The prospects of a fair trial are important: Hoare at [60]. The Limitation Acts are designed to protect defendants from the injustice of having to fight stale claims, especially when any witnesses the defendant might have been able to rely on are not available or have no recollection and there are no documents to assist the court in deciding what was done or not done and why: Donovan at 479A; Robinson at [32]; Adams at [55]. It is, therefore, particularly relevant whether, and to what extent, the defendant's ability to defend the claim has been prejudiced by the lapse of time because of the absence of relevant witnesses and documents: Robinson at [33]; Adams at [55]; Hoare at [50].

7) Subject to considerations of proportionality (as outlined in (11) below), the defendant only deserves to have the obligation to pay due damages removed if the passage of time has significantly diminished the opportunity to defend the claim on liability or amount: Cain v Francis [2008] EWCA Civ 1451, [2009] QB 754, at [69].

8) It is the period after the expiry of the limitation period which is referred to in sub-subsections 33(3)(a) and (b) and carries particular weight: Donovan at 478G. The court may also, however, have regard to the period of delay from the time at which section 14(2) was satisfied until the claim was first notified: Donovan at 478H and 479H-480C; Cain at [74]. The disappearance of evidence and the loss of cogency of evidence even before the limitation clock starts to tick is also relevant, although to a lesser degree: Collins v Secretary of State for Business Innovation and Skills [2014] EWCA Civ 717, [2014] PIQR P19, at [65].

9) The reason for delay is relevant and may affect the balancing exercise. If it has arisen for an excusable reason, it may be fair and just that the action should proceed despite some unfairness to the defendant due to the delay. If, on the other hand, the reasons for the delay or its length are not good ones, that may tip the balance in the other direction: Cain at [73]. I consider that the latter may be better expressed by saying that, if there are no good reasons for the delay or its length, there is nothing to qualify or temper the prejudice which has been caused to the defendant by the effect of the delay on the defendant's ability to defendant the claim.

10) Delay caused by the conduct of the claimant's advisers rather than by the claimant may be excusable in this context: Corbin v Penfold Company Limited [2000] Lloyd's Rep Med 247.

11) In the context of reasons for delay, it is relevant to consider under sub-section 33(3)(a) whether knowledge or information was reasonably suppressed by the claimant which, if not suppressed, would have led to the proceedings being issued earlier, even though the explanation is irrelevant for meeting the objective standard or test in section 14(2) and (3) and so insufficient to prevent the commencement of the limitation period: Hoare at [44]-[45] and [70].

12) Proportionality is material to the exercise of the discretion: Robinson at [32] and [33]; Adams at [54] and [55]. In that context, it may be relevant that the claim has only a thin prospect of success (McGhie at [48]), that the claim is modest in financial terms so as to give rise to disproportionate legal costs (Robinson at [33]; Adams at [55]); McGhie at [48]), that the claimant would have a clear case against his or her solicitors (Donovan at 479F), and, in a personal injury case, the extent and degree of damage to the claimant's health, enjoyment of life and employability (Robinson at [33]; Adams at [55])".

Accordingly, it is plain that the guiding principle under section 33 is one of equity in all the circumstances.

The main issue which often affects asbestos claims is delay and the impact of prejudice on a Defendant's ability to defend the claim fully. Delay is often inevitable where parties have to investigate claims going back decades, and this is a feature of asbestos litigation. In a recent appeal before the High Court in a pleural thickening claim arising from alleged asbestos exposure, Gregory v H J Haynes Limited [2020] EWHC 911 (Ch), Mr Justice Mann stated as follows on the particular issue of delay and section 33 discretion[2]:

2 Paras 20 and 21

> *"The degree and nature of prejudice likely to be suffered by either party as a result of delay is actually a question of fact. The prejudice to the claimant in not being to bring his claim is obvious. The prejudice to the defendant in being deprived of a limitation defence is equally obvious though less relevant as a single factor. What is more significant is the prejudicial effect of the delays that have occurred in this matter.*
>
> *The main prejudicial effect is likely to be the loss of evidence over the years. In the present case such evidence as there was demonstrated, perhaps not surprisingly, that little evidence seemed now to be available to the defendant. The evidence of the defendant (through their solicitor Ms Manners) demonstrated that attempts had been made to contact those who had been directors of the defendant at the time of Mr Gregory's employment and subsequently, and inquiries revealed that they were all dead or untraceable. Most of those who had died had done so even before 2008. No company documents have survived the dissolution of the company, and her efforts had apparently not revealed anyone who could give evidence of working practices at the time of Mr Gregory's employment. That, of itself, gives rise to significant disadvantage to the defendant in meeting the claim."*

Those issues of delay are there in every claim, but the issue which will prove decisive in most cases will be whether the delay is culpable to a party, and whether that delay caused additional prejudice to a Defendant over and above that which they would have suffered in any event. In Gregory, Mr Justice Mann found that the delay in identifying the Defendant's insurers – which had caused the Claimant to delay issuing for fear there would be no pot to meet any damages he may be awarded – was not the Claimant's fault for which he could be culpable. Additionally, and in any event, the delay caused no additional prejudice to the Defendant than they would have faced had he commenced his action within 3 years of becoming symptomatic. As such, the original trial judges' refusal of section 33 discretion was reversed and the claim permitted to proceed[3]:

> *"In a case where the claimant could not reasonably be expected to have commenced a claim for a large part of that period, it is pertinent to consider the extent of this prejudice across elements of the period. It seems to me that the thrust of what the judge below found was that by the time one gets to 2011, or 2014, the damage to the defendant's evidential case had been done in terms of lost evidence. There seemed to be no witnesses left. The judge's paragraph 46 suggests a degradation in the last 9 years. That does not seem to be based on evidence. I suspect that it was more based on judicial instinct that another 9 years makes a bad position worse. Whether or not that is true depends on how bad the position was at the beginning of that 9 years, and the answer seems to be that it was pretty bad by then anyway.*
>
> *In any event, I do not think that the last 9 years is as significant a period as the period since 2014. If one asks the question whether there has been additional prejudice to the defendant in that more recent period (relevant because 2014 is the first point of a time at which one can fairly say the claimant ought to have sued) then I think the answer is that there has not been. By then the damage to the defendant's evidential case has been done."*

A recent example of an asbestosis and diffuse pleural thickening claim in which the Court refused to exercise the statutory discretion in the Claimant's favour was Fudge v. Hawkins and Holmes Limited [2018] EWHC (QB). The claim was issued 5 ½ years out of time. The Court found that the Claimant had not acted reasonably or promptly. Further, inevitably, the Claimant's own memory had got worse, which the Learned Judge found was exacerbated by the Claimant's own destruction of the only available contemporary documentary material which may have supported or undermined his case. Accordingly, even in the context of a case where there was a lengthy period of time before the primary limitation period expired, the further delay since the expiry

3 Paras 24 and 25

of the primary limitation period had, in the Learned Judge' view, resulted in a significant loss of cogency in the evidence.

As was made clear in the asbestos-induced lung cancer claim of Collins v. Secretary of State for Business Innovation and Skills [2014] EWCA Civ 717, the Court must have regard to the effect of the time elapsed before the Claimant's "*date of knowledge*" as one of the relevant factors, but less weight should be accorded to any prejudice accruing in this period than to prejudice accruing after the expiry of the primary limitation period, which is the factor listed specifically in Section 33.

Accordingly, section 33 ought to be seen as a contentious area for all parties. The nature of asbestos-related injuries, and the large awards of damages which they attract, together with the suffering which Claimant's go through are strong factors in any assessment of whether or not it will be equitable to grant section 33 discretion. For partly the same reason, so too is prejudice which a Defendant can ascribe to a Claimant's delay. Evidencing culpable delay and consequential prejudice – together with a chronology of when that prejudice likely occurred – is therefore imperative evidence for a Court which both parties should focus on. Naturally, a Claimant will seek to minimise any culpable delay on their part and any prejudice arising (as happened in *Gregory*), whilst a Defendant will seek to do the opposite.

(iii) Fatal claims

(a) Claims under the Law Reform (Miscellaneous) Provisions Act 1934 on behalf of the estate

Under Section 11(5) of the Limitation Act 1980, the first question is whether or not the claim was still in time at the point of death. That is analysed as above. If the claim was out of time at death, the claim is statute-barred and can only proceed, if at all, under Section 33.

On the other hand, if the claim was still in time at the moment of death, the "*limitation clock*" re-starts, and the limitation period is as follows:-

> *"If the person injured dies before the expiration of the period mentioned in subsection (4) above, the period applicable as respects the cause of action surviving for the benefit of his estate by virtue of section 1 of the Law Reform (Miscellaneous Provisions) Act 1934 shall be three years from—*
>
> *(a) the date of death; or*
>
> *(b) the date of the personal representative's knowledge;*
>
> *whichever is the later".*

"*Knowledge*" is as addressed in Section 14 above.

If and insofar as Section 33 does apply, the principles are as addressed above.

(b) **Claims under the Fatal Accidents Act 1976**

Under Section 12(1) of the 1976 Act:

> "*(1) an action under the Fatal Accidents Act 1976 shall not be brought if the death occurred when the person injured could no longer maintain an action and recover damages in respect of the injury (whether because of a time limit in this Act or in any other Act, or for any other reason). Where any such action by the injured person would have been barred by the time limit in section 11 or 11A of this Act, no account shall be taken of the possibility of that time limit being overridden under section 33 of this Act*".

On a plain reading this appears to suggest that if the time for the Deceased to being a claim had expired by the time of death, no claim can be brought under the 1976 Act. This, however, is an incorrect interpretation because of Section 33(2) of the 1980 Act:-

> "*The court shall not under this section disapply section 12(1) except where the reason why the person injured could no longer maintain an*

> *action was because of the time limit in section 11 or subsection (4) of section 11A*".

If the claim was still in time at the date of death, then the time limit for the 1976 Act claim to be brought is set out in Section 12(2) of the 1980 Act:-

> "*(2) None of the time limits given in the preceding provisions of this Act shall apply to an action under the Fatal Accidents Act 1976, but no such action shall be brought after the expiration of three years from—*
>
> *(a) the date of death; or*
>
> *(b) the date of knowledge of the person for whose benefit the action is brought;*
>
> *whichever is the later*".

If and insofar as Section 33 does apply (whether because the claim of the Deceased would have been out of time at the date of death, or because the time limit in Section 12(2) for a 1976 Act claim was missed), the principles are as addressed above.

(iv) Conclusions

Limitation has proven to be a fertile source of dispute in asbestos litigation, with, as set out above, there being decisions to support both the Claimant and the Defendant on "*date of knowledge*" and whether or not an out-of-time claim should be permitted to proceed.

MORE BOOKS BY LAW BRIEF PUBLISHING

A selection of our other titles available now:-

- 'Covid-19, Homeworking and the Law – The Essential Guide to Employment and GDPR Issues' by Forbes Solicitors
- 'Covid-19, Force Majeure and Frustration of Contracts – The Essential Guide' by Keith Markham
- 'Covid-19 and Criminal Law – The Essential Guide' by Ramya Nagesh
- 'Covid-19 and Family Law in England and Wales – The Essential Guide' by Safda Mahmood
- 'Covid-19 and the Implications for Planning Law – The Essential Guide' by Bob Mc Geady & Meyric Lewis
- 'Covid-19, Residential Property, Equity Release and Enfranchisement – The Essential Guide' by Paul Sams and Louise Uphill
- 'Covid-19, Brexit and the Law of Commercial Leases – The Essential Guide' by Mark Shelton
- 'Covid-19 and the Law Relating to Food in the UK and Republic of Ireland – The Essential Guide' by Ian Thomas
- 'A Practical Guide to the General Data Protection Regulation (GDPR) – 2nd Edition' by Keith Markham
- 'Ellis on Credit Hire – Sixth Edition' by Aidan Ellis & Tim Kevan
- 'A Practical Guide to Working with Litigants in Person and McKenzie Friends in Family Cases' by Stuart Barlow
- 'Protecting Unregistered Brands: A Practical Guide to the Law of Passing Off' by Lorna Brazell
- 'A Practical Guide to Secondary Liability and Joint Enterprise Post-Jogee' by Joanne Cecil & James Mehigan

'A Practical Guide to the Pre-Action RTA Claims Protocol for Personal Injury Lawyers' by Antonia Ford
'A Practical Guide to Neighbour Disputes and the Law' by Alexander Walsh
'A Practical Guide to Forfeiture of Leases' by Mark Shelton
'A Practical Guide to Coercive Control for Legal Practitioners and Victims' by Rachel Horman
'A Practical Guide to Rights Over Airspace and Subsoil' by Daniel Gatty
'Tackling Disclosure in the Criminal Courts – A Practitioner's Guide' by Narita Bahra QC & Don Ramble
'A Practical Guide to the Law of Driverless Cars – Second Edition' by Alex Glassbrook, Emma Northey & Scarlett Milligan
'A Practical Guide to TOLATA Claims' by Greg Williams
'Artificial Intelligence – The Practical Legal Issues' by John Buyers
'A Practical Guide to the Law of Prescription in Scotland' by Andrew Foyle
'A Practical Guide to the Construction and Rectification of Wills and Trust Instruments' by Edward Hewitt
'A Practical Guide to the Law of Bullying and Harassment in the Workplace' by Philip Hyland
'How to Be a Freelance Solicitor: A Practical Guide to the SRA-Regulated Freelance Solicitor Model' by Paul Bennett
'A Practical Guide to Prison Injury Claims' by Malcolm Johnson
'A Practical Guide to the Small Claims Track' by Dominic Bright
'A Practical Guide to Advising Clients at the Police Station' by Colin Stephen McKeown-Beaumont
'A Practical Guide to Antisocial Behaviour Injunctions' by Iain Wightwick
'Practical Mediation: A Guide for Mediators, Advocates, Advisers, Lawyers, and Students in Civil, Commercial, Business, Property, Workplace, and Employment Cases' by Jonathan Dingle with John Sephton
'The Mini-Pupillage Workbook' by David Boyle

'A Practical Guide to Crofting Law' by Brian Inkster
'A Practical Guide to Spousal Maintenance' by Liz Cowell
'A Practical Guide to the Law of Domain Names and Cybersquatting' by Andrew Clemson
'A Practical Guide to the Law of Gender Pay Gap Reporting' by Harini Iyengar
'A Practical Guide to the Rights of Grandparents in Children Proceedings' by Stuart Barlow
'NHS Whistleblowing and the Law' by Joseph England
'Employment Law and the Gig Economy' by Nigel Mackay & Annie Powell
'A Practical Guide to Noise Induced Hearing Loss (NIHL) Claims' by Andrew Mckie, Ian Skeate, Gareth McAloon
'An Introduction to Beauty Negligence Claims – A Practical Guide for the Personal Injury Practitioner' by Greg Almond
'Intercompany Agreements for Transfer Pricing Compliance' by Paul Sutton
'Zen and the Art of Mediation' by Martin Plowman
'A Practical Guide to the SRA Principles, Individual and Law Firm Codes of Conduct 2019 – What Every Law Firm Needs to Know' by Paul Bennett
'A Practical Guide to Adoption for Family Lawyers' by Graham Pegg
'A Practical Guide to Industrial Disease Claims' by Andrew Mckie & Ian Skeate
'A Practical Guide to Redundancy' by Philip Hyland
'A Practical Guide to Vicarious Liability' by Mariel Irvine
'A Practical Guide to Applications for Landlord's Consent and Variation of Leases' by Mark Shelton
'A Practical Guide to Relief from Sanctions Post-Mitchell and Denton' by Peter Causton
'A Practical Guide to Equity Release for Advisors' by Paul Sams
'A Practical Guide to Unlawful Eviction and Harassment' by Stephanie Lovegrove
'A Practical Guide to the Law Relating to Food' by Ian Thomas

'A Practical Guide to Financial Services Claims' by Chris Hegarty

'The Law of Houses in Multiple Occupation: A Practical Guide to HMO Proceedings' by Julian Hunt

'A Practical Guide to Unlawful Eviction and Harassment' by Stephanie Lovegrove

'A Practical Guide to Solicitor and Client Costs' by Robin Dunne

'Occupiers, Highways and Defective Premises Claims: A Practical Guide Post-Jackson – 2nd Edition' by Andrew Mckie

'A Practical Guide to Financial Ombudsman Service Claims' by Adam Temple & Robert Scrivenor

'A Practical Guide to Advising Schools on Employment Law' by Jonathan Holden

'A Practical Guide to Running Housing Disrepair and Cavity Wall Claims: 2nd Edition' by Andrew Mckie & Ian Skeate

'A Practical Guide to Holiday Sickness Claims – 2nd Edition' by Andrew Mckie & Ian Skeate

'Arguments and Tactics for Personal Injury and Clinical Negligence Claims' by Dorian Williams

'A Practical Guide to QOCS and Fundamental Dishonesty' by James Bentley

'A Practical Guide to Drone Law' by Rufus Ballaster, Andrew Firman, Eleanor Clot

'A Practical Guide to Compliance for Personal Injury Firms Working With Claims Management Companies' by Paul Bennett

'A Practical Guide to the Landlord and Tenant Act 1954: Commercial Tenancies' by Richard Hayes & David Sawtell

'A Practical Guide to Dog Law for Owners and Others' by Andrea Pitt

'RTA Allegations of Fraud in a Post-Jackson Era: The Handbook – 2nd Edition' by Andrew Mckie

'RTA Personal Injury Claims: A Practical Guide Post-Jackson' by Andrew Mckie

'On Experts: CPR35 for Lawyers and Experts' by David Boyle

'An Introduction to Personal Injury Law' by David Boyle

www.ingramcontent.com/pod-product-compliance
Lightning Source LLC
LaVergne TN
LVHW022047200926
848481LV00003B/813